Love, A Guide to Advancing Your Soul

Love, A Guide to Advancing Your Soul

Elizabeth Villani

BOOKS

Winchester, UK
Washington, USA

First published by O-Books, 2011
O-Books is an imprint of John Hunt Publishing Ltd., Laurel House, Station Approach,
Alresford, Hants, SO24 9JH, UK
office1@o-books.net
www.o-books.com

For distributor details and how to order please visit the 'Ordering' section on our website.

Text copyright: Elizabeth Villani 2010

ISBN: 978 1 84694 710 0

A CIP catalogue record for this book is available from the British Library.

Design: Stuart Davies

Printed in the UK by CPI Antony Rowe
Printed in the USA by Offset Paperback Mfrs, Inc

We operate a distinctive and ethical publishing philosophy in all
areas of our business, from our global network of authors to
production and worldwide distribution.

CONTENTS

Also by Elizabeth Villani

Awakening

Awakening is easy, in just 69 pages you can awaken your soul and be who you really are. The soul may awaken you or you may awaken yourself. The world is awakening. For some it can be a painful experience, for others shocking and surprising but it can be a conscious choice. A choice to live a greater life, awakened to the truth.

www.elizabethvillani.net

For Nicole and for every beautiful soul that walks upon our earth.

Foreword

by Dr Robert Holden

I think everyone should write a book about love at least once in a lifetime. If not a book, at least a poem or a song. Everything you do in your life is motivated by a desire, on some level, to know love, to extend love, and to be loved. Love is the primary purpose of your life. Love is what you are busy about; even when it may look like you are busy with something else. Everyone has a book about love somewhere inside themselves.

Elizabeth Villani has written a book about love. Elizabeth tells us that she is an ordinary person, just like you and me. She speaks intimately to us about the story of her life, the highs and lows, the dark and the light. As you turn the pages of her book, you witness a person who is gaining a beautiful awareness of what it really means to love and be loved. "Our natural state is love," she writes. "You know it. I know it. We all know it. Now we all need to be it."

Reading a book about love is almost as good as writing one yourself. I think everyone should read a book about love at least once in a lifetime. If not a book, at least a poem or a song. Reading about love helps you to tune in to your true nature. It plugs you in consciously to the wisdom of your heart. It activates something in you that makes you want to be even more loving, and literally be the presence of love in your life.

As you turn the pages of Elizabeth's book, I encourage you to keep asking yourself *how can I live this today?*

Elizabeth has shown us through her story, that we can all tap into a higher consciousness of love and translate that natural inspiration into our own life. Remember, love is our natural state. This means that, deep down, you already know how to love and be loved. Love is not a technique you learn, a skill to be acquired, or a secret you find on the last page of a book; it is a natural ability that flows effortlessly through you when you are willing to let it.

I am convinced that the purpose of your life is to love and be loved. Nothing else matters quite as much. I believe that reading Elizabeth's book will help you to fulfill your purpose. What a gift Elizabeth has given us. Thank you Elizabeth. I hope you will smile occasionally at the thought of how your book has blessed your life and all your readers' lives too. Love really is a blessing. Love blesses us all.

With Love,
Robert Holden
author of *Shift Happens!*

Acknowledgements

A big thank you to every soul that has ever stepped into my path, this book is the result of many souls and circumstances all aligning in love to propel it out to the world.

I would like to thank my publisher O-Books for knowing its importance and Robert Holden for his amazing kindness and support for my work. My great friends Lisa Gates and Lisa Whitehead who have both spurred me on to share our truth and without whom this guide would not have been written.

Thank you to Nicola Hack whose love and massage supported the sharing of our great truth and to Richard Edwards for making mediumship so powerfully clear for me.

I would like to express my love and thanks to all of my clients, you have played such an enormous role in my life and have been an inspiration, I wish each of you truth, happiness and success.

The wonderful children of Ropsley school, thank you sharing your hearts with me and the world for an hour. Thank you for sharing such a divine surprise!

My parents and my guides, thank you.

Jerome, thank you for your unconditional love, faith and belief.

Nicole, may you always walk with joy in every footstep.

A prayer from St Francis

Make me a channel of your peace.
Where there is hatred let me bring your love;
Where there is injury, your pardon, Lord;
And where there's doubt, true faith in you:

Oh, Master, grant that I may never seek
So much to be consoled as to console;
To be understood as to understand;
To be loved, as to love with all my soul.

Make me a channel of your peace.
Where there's despair in life, let me bring hope;
Where there is darkness, only light;
And where there's sadness, ever joy:

Make me a channel of your peace.
It is in pardoning that we are pardoned,
In giving of ourselves that we receive,
And in dying that we're born to eternal life.

I am a little pencil in the hand of a writing God who is sending a love letter to the world.

Mother Teresa

In December 2008 I experienced an amazing spiritual vision, a divine calling. I was shown the truth. In a state of absolute calm during a massage I was shown the world, myself, all of us, and what "this" is all about. I was shown in magical pictures how each soul comes to this world with lessons to remember, and to evolve. We live our lives as if in a huge playground, unaware of this. We are born again and again until we begin to live in truth, to fully experience and express the love that we are.

Only then do we advance our soul and reach our own karmic enlightenment.

Preface

In life we are taught to adhere to sets of rules and principles that govern our lands.

We are also taught a culture and a set of behaviors and requirements that we are expected to conform to.

We spend our lives striving to fit the bill.

We fall for the illusion.

In falling we express our amnesia.

We take part in the play only to return to the stage again and again until we awaken. Leaving lives scattered with fear.

So what if all of this was an illusion?

What if you are a soul on a karmic journey?

What if you have been given chance after chance after chance to get it right?

What if the real teaching occurred before you got here in this body?

What if you experienced lessons of love at the gates to earth?

What if your purpose here is to advance your soul by remembering, expressing and living those lessons?

What if the illusion that you live in is wrong?

What if this life really is about forgiving and giving to others and in doing so this world automatically brings you opportunities to receive?

What if you are an immortal soul who only knows the real truth when you die at the end of your life here?

What if this is how it works?

Would you be ready to take the chance to work to advance your soul?

Introduction

You have lived many lives. You are here to experience the wonder of your soul, the wonder of existence, the wonder of life. You are here to joyfully create anything that you wish. Wherever you are in your life right now you have this most amazing choice. Do you choose to surrender and lay down your negative old ways, or will you continue the battle, again and again and again?

More and more of us are awakening. The message of our awakening is simple. We have to wake up. We have to stop homogenising our consciousness with wall to wall TV and other mindless activity. We have to consciously look at ourselves and our worlds with eyes wide open and believe that good is what we can then choose to see. We have to believe in ourselves and open up our consciousness to remembering and learning a new way of existing. And yet this new way is actually the old way. We just can't remember it.

We are living in a time of great awakening and most of us are asking questions...questions about what to do, who to be, what "this" is all about.

I have been shown the answer, the answer is love.

If you have come to this book before reading "Awakening" I recommend that you read it too. Until you have truly awoken, you will always have the challenge of your human ego, your perceptions, your self talk getting in your way.

In order to be truly happy, you have to make this a good, honest and happy perception, one that you deserve and can consciously have. You just have to decide to go and grab it.

Once we have awoken, the curiosity really begins. We want to remember. We want to progress and know the truth of who we are and what this life is really about.

So who are you?

Once you have realized that you are not the summation of your thoughts or generations of your family or the image that you portray, you want to know who you really are.

I contemplated this question for some time and what I realized quite simply is that I am me. The "me" that was always there under the mask that I put on to get through life. The "me" that was at times buried under all of that doing and self doubting! The "me" that couldn't sell bric-a-brac to old ladies when I was seven because I cried at the thought of taking their money from them. The "me" that understands others and is two million per cent emotional and sensitive. The me that I sometimes hide. No matter what I think I should or shouldn't be. No matter what others think that I should or shouldn't be. Without politics, religion, social conformity, requirements and demands. Simply, truthfully, me. And you are you.

We have one mission. To be us. The very best us that we possibly can be. To let us as we really are help ourselves and others to express ourselves in love.

We are here to express and advance our souls to the point where we never have to enter this third dimension again, or at least not because we still have much to become. We will choose to come here to experience creation, to create a physical world of love.

To do this, to become truly us, we need to look and live from within, from the inside out. We have to consciously open our hearts to the love and feelings right at the core of us. We must learn to remember who we truly are and not conform and be distracted. We must gently move out of living through our heads and park our consciousness firmly in our hearts.

We have to believe that this, just this, is enough and trust that this is what this life is all about.

As I turn myself inside out I know with absolute certainty that I was born into this world to feel and demonstrate deep love. It's me. As a child I cannot describe enough in these words what being me "felt" like. To say it simply, I didn't think, I felt. As a child I cried and cried...and then I cried some more. No amount of logic deterred me from my feelings. My heart was my voice, and it still is. It has been covered up slightly from conditioning, western education and culture, not to mention a good 15 years conforming to society's vision of success, but there the magic remains.

Our world is accelerating. We juggle with speed. We list. We panic. We hide. We strive to keep up and fit in. Most of us conform. We become the people that society and our parents mould us to be. We analyse and think our way through our days. When things feel great it reflects our success. When they don't we either hide and blame or take a tablet and give up. We gossip. We back stab. We beat ourselves up. We blame. We are at times fuelled by hatred and fear and jealousy.

Millions of us have lost our capacity for joy. We have forgotten how to love. We have forgotten who we are. We spend our time discussing the lives and the comings and goings of others. Our focus is on what we can see with our eyes, not with our hearts. Bitterness, anger, resentment are the products.

This does not have to be so. Love is free. It is there for everyone. It is powerful. It feels wonderful. It heals. It surprises. It governs the sacred laws of the lands. It lifts away the shadows and leaves a healthy spiritual, open and supportive human being. Its wonderful power enlightens not only the giver but the receiver too. Love is a choice. Love is you.

It never ceases to astonish me when people close their hearts to everyday compassion and kindness. Conscious love as a way of life is awe inspiring. Yes, it heals the world, but you know feeling and being kindness, forgiveness, acceptance, feels good. It feels good as you open your door at night after your day. It feels good to wake up excited by the feeling of happiness and joy that comes from consciously deciding that love is the answer. You are the answer.

This is the pathway to advancing your soul.

My belief today is the same as Kuan Yin. This beautiful ascended master believed that kindness and forgiveness give the human spirit the power to ascend. In other words, the power to lift the vibrational energy of your soul. Kuan Yin made it her earthly purpose to end the cycles of soul reincarnation by teaching that through living by kindness and forgiveness, the soul reaches enlightenment, so stopping the need to incarnate because the lessons have been learnt and lived.

If this guide helps you to live a more fulfilling life and stand closer to the joy of your experience here when you pass back to spirit, then I will feel that I have helped this adventure to be an easier, more loving experience for you.

Even if you find it difficult to see how the changes in this book will help your income, or your career, know that by becoming more loving you are creating a life in which you and others can experience real growth. At a soul level you don't need material success. You don't need to be the boss, the director, the doer. You are simply here to experience love and grow within it.

You hold the power within you to be part of the generation that makes the biggest step. The ones who saw the pearls of wisdom and laid them down as stepping stones to ascension. To the wonder of the truth. Heaven on earth, for all to experience.

So this is my purpose, to write this book to teach each heart in our world how to advance their soul. To lay out the lessons to be remembered and expressed. To review what this means for you and look at what steps you can take to move your soul forward in your current life.

I give you these words to help you to be the very best person that you can be. To speak your truth. To stick to being the very best of you. To let go of self consciousness and live this life as a perfect expression of love.

CHAPTER ONE

OUR TRUE REALITY

What is the meaning of life?

Until I experienced that amazing mystical vision, 1 thought that our reality was one of two things. Either simply a life to be lived, then we die and that's that, or secondly, a life that was to be lived well, that is overseen and supported by some kind of God and heaven who, when we die, judges how well we have done. Just like you, I suspect.

I recently watched the Monty Python film "The Meaning of Life" (1983). Fascinating and very funny in parts, though not to everyone's taste, the film sets out to answer this question: what is the meaning of life? Each sketch offers the viewer different and entertaining ideas and perspectives. At one point, towards the end of the film, the cast is sat in a large corporate boardroom, dressed in business suits like office executives, and they act out a sketch which really strikes me – had they got it right?

Large corporate boardroom filled with suited executives...

Exec 1, Item six on the agenda: "The Meaning of Life" Now uh, Harry, you've had some thoughts on this?

Exec 2, I've had a team working on this over the past few weeks, and what we've come up with can be reduced to two fundamental concepts. One: People aren't wearing enough hats. Two: Matter is energy. In the universe there are many energy fields which we cannot normally perceive. Some energies have a spiritual source which act upon a person's soul. However, this "soul" does not exist as initio as orthodox Christianity teaches; it has to be brought into existence by a process of guided self-observation. However, this is rarely achieved owing to man's unique ability to be distracted from spiritual matters by everyday trivia.

Exec 3, What was that about hats again?

Exec 2, Oh, Uh... people aren't wearing enough.

Exec 1, Is this true?

Exec 4, Certainly. Hat sales have increased but not pari passu, as our research...

Exec 3, [*Interrupting*] "Not wearing enough"? enough for what purpose?

 Exec 5, Can I just ask, with reference to your second point, when you say souls don't develop because people become distracted...

[*looking out window*]

The mystical experience showed that I was wrong, and that they were right!

We are souls having a human experience, but we don't realize it because we get distracted.

The years and months leading up to the mystical vision led to the opening of my channel.

In May 2008 my beloved grandmother Margaret died. At 95 she had lead a full life, and yet as we know when someone that we love dies we can feel a terrible loss. The day that she died I was in southern England attending a Christening. During the service the hymn "Make me a channel of your peace" was sung. I sat tears pouring down my face sending my Grandmother reiki healing in what were to be her final hours.

A week later at her funeral the same hymn rang out in her memory. From then on it was all that I could hear. I sang it in the shower. I hummed it throughout my days. It was the backdrop to my dreams. I began to let go and let God. Each day I would focus on what I could give. What I was guided through my intuition to do. I allowed myself to let go of the how. I asked for guidance.

I had spent many years gently cleaning my spirit of hurt and resentment. I had become an expert on positivity and the power of an empowered mind. I had trained in reiki and accessed intuitive powers through my work with people and through silent contemplation. I decided to let grace lead me to where I was meant to be and I longed for a direct connection, a calling, and yet I didn't demand it, or even really think about it that much when I look back, it was just gently asked. It was answered.

In December that year, I lay on a bed in a beauty salon just down the road from my home and my life changed forever. I went for a stone massage with a reiki trained therapist who I have come to know over the years. I lay on the bed looking forward to what had always been a relaxing and comforting experience.

What happened next was astounding. As clear as day I was shown our true reality. I was shown the earth and heaven all around it. I was shown that souls come here to remember and develop to live lives centered in love. I was shown that some of us come here as teachers to support and induce love in others and in our world. I was shown that I was being switched on, woken up to my true purpose. My role was shown to me. I was a midwife to the spirit. I was shown that I was to apply the methods that I had developed and the person inside that I am, to help each individual to awaken their soul and then live in love. I was shown that the trip that I was just about to depart on to New Zealand and Hong Kong was not just about my work and my family, but about stretching my perception of the world, so that I could successfully apply the message of the vision to help all of us, no matter where on earth we lived. I was shown people in my life and their role and how they would help. I was shown that I was a spiritual guide and teacher and I was invited to begin.

Nikki, the therapist, had no idea that this was all going on and after the massage, as you can imagine, I was rather spaced out! I felt a love and a knowing and a serenity that I had never experienced before and although my logical mind questioned what I had just experienced, I knew without any doubt that I had just been shown the truth. I had been shown directly by source, by god, by an amazing and beautiful power, what all of "this" is about.

When I left the salon I had to go straight to a children's party at "Crazy Bongos" – one of these huge indoor playgrounds for the under tens which are full of screaming children and stressed parents! My daughter had been invited to a friend's birthday party and I sat there in a daze, looking at all of the people there and it struck me what an enormous task laid head. They had no idea. Not only did they have no idea but if I told these people what I had just seen then they would have branded me a lunatic!

I kept it to myself and went off on the trip.

Now what I want you to realize is that I am a normal grounded human being. I didn't see spirits as a child. I spent eight years of my life sat at a desk on the London treadmill. I run my own business going into factories and offices and teaching people to be themselves and with it successful and happier. I am a mother, a wife, a daughter. I make spaghetti bolognese and do the ironing. I pay my taxes and live what is considered, a normal life. I really am not some whacko!

Before the vision I had not read spiritual books. This whole spiritual thing was completely new to me. I had never heard of Eckhart Tolle or Neale Donald Walsh. Doreen Virtue was vaguely familiar from the pack of angel cards that I had bought a few years earlier, but really I had never come across any of that stuff. As a teenager I used to play with tarot and I have always been interested in astrology. But they were never the center of my life. More a hobby and a bit of fun.

What I am trying to convey then is that I am just like you.

When I wrote my first book "Awakening," I had no idea what some of what I was writing meant. Since writing it I have researched and read and been astonished that others hold the same vision of our true reality. Many famous authors have written books and give talks around the same truth. The same truth that I was shown. The truth that our true reality is not what most of us think.

Our true reality is one where we are all souls that are connected. We are reincarnated here on this earth, in this dimension, spirits having a physical experience. The people around us in our lives are pre-chosen, as are our challenges and life circumstances. All set up so that we have the best chance of remembering and experiencing our lessons, who we really are. We have also volunteered to help others to do the same. We are all connected to each other as one source, whether you call that God, or source, or spirit or any other name. Our true reality is that this life is temporary. It is a joyful opportunity to express and share who we really are. But most of us have no idea.

When my grandmother died I felt closer to her than when she was physically alive. I can talk to her within myself and I know that she is listening. Every time that I talk to her the hairs stand up on the back of my neck and an energy, warm and tingly, enters my body from behind me. She loved life and my sense is that she is already here again, already re-born.

We are surrounded by helpers and supporters, whether you sense angels, guides, spirits or your dead loved ones. All you have to do is ask and they are right there with you. You are a hugely powerful, intuitive expression of energy. You are pure love. You access these powers through love. Once awoken, once you begin living not through your self-conscious, judgmental head, but through your heart, you experience your karmic lessons and advance your soul. It is this that tells us whether we have succeeded in life, not the size of our bank balance or the number of cars in our drive. It is through love that we live a life that has been truly lived.

There is a common aspect on which many experts on the

afterlife agree, the life review. In the loving arms of your soul group, each soul on returning home reviews the impact of their recent three dimensional life. They see their lessons and reactions to them. They review their progress against what they aimed to do and give and they look at the wider ripples of their earthly life in this vibration.

Now I am absolutely certain that, like me, you want to be at that life review and feel good. You want to be there and share all of the loving words, thoughts, feelings and gestures that you gave in your life, both to yourself and your soul and to that of others. You want your heart to fill with pride.

You will not want to stand there and cry soulful tears of shame, guilt, and regret.

I would feel real anger and disappointment at myself and earthly embarrassment if I was sharing and watching a load of awful things that I had done to myself and others. Then the icing on the cake, the realisation that I had to go and try again. There is no escape from your negative action on yourself and others. And only joy in the positives.

The great thing is that you can choose right now to know that when you review your life with the support of your fellow loving souls that you did it, the best that you could do. You reached enlightenment! Your loving actions and self care taught you all of the lessons of the soul. You lived your love and spread a beautiful wave bigger than you could ever comprehend. You can now feel the truth of love fully envelope your soul.

Want to be there?

So our true reality is exposed. This book is being published to support you in lifting your consciousness so that you awaken to and express your true reality, your true self now. The more of us that awaken now and lift our vibration, the greater the impact on our group consciousness and our planet. 2012 is seen by many as the gateway to a new human reality. A new world age. The Mayans predicted it in their calendar and many books and articles have been written about it. We are in a time of new beginnings, of a new, unfolding way of living, a new level of consciousness. What is the difference between the new world age and the old one? Love. At this time in our reality, as we stand here incarnated on this earth, we have the opportunity to lift our vibration. How? By awakening to who we really are and moving away from self doubt, negatives and materialism and moving towards a life of joy and inner power. A life expressed through love.

It's a wonderful, grounded feeling to know that "yes, there is more to life".

Now it's our time to live it.

At the end of each chapter in this guide I have listed a selection of affirmations that sum up the learnings for you. You can speak and feel these affirmations and refer back to them to help you to advance your soul through the lessons of love. By choosing the path of love, the true reality, you will bring the lessons into being in your life right now. You will become and express who you really are.

CHAPTER TWO

THE SPIRITUAL FACTS OF LIFE

We live our lives reincarnating again and again. We come back in each life to learn and express the same lessons. As souls we are looking for purity of expression. We are aiming for a life full of moments that ignite and enlighten our existence, that will move us forward to a greater level of soul evolution. We are all at varying levels of advancement. Those with the greatest journey are living lives full of anger, fear and resentment. A living hell. Those further along the path are living lives sprinkled with happiness. They are giving to others, have integrity, are examples of goodness in our societies. Our opportunity here, in this life, is to advance towards the latter.

No matter how advanced your soul, there are a set of spiritual facts that underpin our true reality here and when we live life remembering them, our journey towards advancement is made easier.

The spiritual facts of life

- ♥ Happiness and joy come from being ourselves at a soul level.
- ♥ Love through forgiveness and kindness opens the heart to learning and experiencing.
- ♥ Our natural state is love.
- ♥ Our life's mission is to be and give of ourselves.
- ♥ As we advance, we journey towards the truth, we live our lives in light, in enlightenment.
- ♥ Enlightenment, the truth, is love.
- ♥ We are love. We are all One.

Let's look at each in turn.

Happiness and joy come from being ourselves at a soul level

We are all walking around wearing a mask. A mask that shows the person that we think we should be and that others expect to see.

When we start out in life we are filled with a sense of strength. We know who we are and in some cases where we want to get to. It is different for different personalities and changes based upon our life's circumstances, but all of us have a knowing, a strength, a core energy inside of us. What then happens is that we start our first job or enrol in our studies, meet new friends and become part of new communities and we want to fit in. We want to be accepted. And so what do we do? We change ourselves to fit. We take on the behaviors of those around us so that we become like them. We fit in. The problem is that when we do this, when we take on the characteristics of others, we start to cover up ourselves and that makes us look unnatural, uncomfortable, and we know it and so what we do to fit the mould and climb the ladder and be accepted is we push harder. We work longer and strive to be a success. What then happens is we become out of balance. All work and no play or we lose focus in our lives. We try to inject humor to get people to like us or bond through talking about things negatively. We become anxious. If you then throw in the culture of materialism, the comparison culture that we all live in as we strive for "perfection", we start to feel like life has happened to us and know inside that we are not good enough. We look for meaning in other ways, even just a nicer sandwich on a Friday lunchtime. All to make ourselves feel better. For some of us, we change jobs, go and have a baby, have a breakdown. But for all of us, we find ourselves feeling a gap, not being happy without knowing why. I have found that some of us go through this cycle several times. But all of us are on the cycle. It's natural. It's human. It's the reason for the gap. You are the gap. How? You are not being who you really are.

No matter what your physical job or role in this life, be it a mother or a factory worker, who you are in essence is your answer to how to fill your days. You do, you are active, but you are not a doing, you are a being. When you focus purely on what you do, you can forget who you are as a being and when you stop doing no one is left. You lose part of yourself and you extinguish your light. Becoming the light that you are, being who you are destroys the darkness. Your light is who you cover up. You at heart, at soul level. The one behind the mask.

People always think that they are what they believe or what they do or don't do. "I am a father." "I am a scientist." "I am not great at maths." "I am a reader." "I am spiritual." "I am an accountant." "I am from South Carolina." "I am a New Zealander." "I am a northerner." You experience all of these things but they are not who you are. They are your chosen vehicle for expressing who you are.

Our general perception before awakening is that we are what we think in our heads. We are our thoughts. But the essence of you never changes. Your thoughts do. You can choose to change your thoughts. You can't choose to change who you actually are at heart, at soul level. Older generations know this. They have the wisdom to now know that they feel the same at 85 on the inside as they did at 25. Their bodies have changed, as have their lives and circumstances. But they "feel" the same. "You are as young as you feel."

Time, role models, self talk, education, culture, all influence your thoughts. They create your library of positive and negative beliefs about yourself and the world around you. You wear your beliefs like a filter. You see through your beliefs and others see you through them as you act them out. Thoughts become things. Have negative expectations of yourself and generally you will get what you expect. Negative thoughts cloud over who you are and generate an internal perception that you are not good enough, fuelling the thoughts that you have to "do more" in order to achieve. Faster. Quicker. Better. Fight! I am not good enough screams your negative self doubt! We all have it...

I have never met anyone without this belief. It makes people hide. It makes them strive. It makes them lie. It makes them cover up who they are inside. It means that you can never be the person that you were born to be, because you would not dare! So you are left with a questioning emptiness. You fill your time back to back with wall to wall TV, doing, comparing. All numbing the pain of the empty question. What is this all about? Addictions in any form numb the senses, as the soul cries and the truth sleeps.

When I run workshops I ask the participants to compliment each other. Do you know that the way that they naturally do this is at a soul level? They can see the soul in the other and this is what they compliment them on. Each of them thinks that they are not good enough. They get self conscious in front of others - we all do when we are not comfortable with ourselves. This is because we perceive that others are judging us, that they think little of us. People's perception of themselves is always significantly less than that of those around them. People around them can see the good and uniqueness within them. They think that they are more than good enough. They may envy them even and compare themselves to them. All whilst the individual is busy hiding and shrinking and getting self conscious by believing that others see them negatively.

Realising that others see them through positive eyes is quite shocking in some cases. Even when presented with ten pieces of really positive personal feedback, the individual always finds it hard to accept that the compliments are real and not just said to make them feel better. They are said to make them feel better but they are also real! What is it that our societies are breeding that generates this response in humans? To think that if we put ourselves down and don't think too much of ourselves then that is right and the way to be liked and to live? What makes us cringe at being told openly how great we are? Why can't we be great?

This smokescreen of modesty that exists does nothing but generate self doubt which leads to self defeating behavior and limited results. We know it and we numb it.

If we can open our minds to perceive that we are good enough, that we are good people, then we open up a channel to our hearts. We don't need to put others down or compare. Because we are good enough. We don't need to back-stab or gossip because we don't need to feel the power of superiority. Our complex is gone! We are ok as we are! And as I will go into later, we are not left with the guilt and negative karma either!

It feels bad when we think little of ourselves and therefore wear masks. We feel frustrated and alone. We feel exhausted and out of answers as the world motors on around us. Happiness is something that we experience in small instants of success. Real happiness seems just out of our reach as yet another lesson comes along to bite us. Others have more happiness than us.

A random act of kindness, the achievement of a goal, feels great, but it doesn't last. Real lasting happiness comes when we allow ourselves to be who we really are. It doesn't mean that life won't throw some challenges at us. Remember that we are here to learn and evolve. But we can accelerate that learning and stop the repeating lessons by opening up to our soul. To ourselves. And let that lead our way.

So happiness and joy come from being yourself, from your soul, your heart. Not your head, where your thoughts live. You are the you that you don't always show. The one that your mother always seems to know! You. Your feelings and natural responses. The one that you think others don't see. Remembering that the answer is you will stop the comparisons and the external striving towards having everything that you think you need in order to be a success and to look a success. Success in this life is found when you start being you, so advancing your soul.

Love through forgiveness and kindness opens the heart to learning and experiencing

Forgiving yourself for your past actions, thoughts and behaviors will free your spirit of guilt, allowing you to open up and accept the person that you are. There is nothing to be gained by beating yourself up. If you were perfect then you wouldn't be here, so accept that you have faults and that you have something to learn. Let go of the guilt and be open to learning. If you think that you know everything, then you'll never learn at all. If you are busy beating yourself up and feeling bad about yourself and what you have or haven't done then you are wearing blinkers. You can't see the opportunities laid in front of you because your focus is on the past.

Everything happens for a reason. You are NOT the one in control and sometimes life deals you a card that can be tough. Tough love is sometimes the best love. Its intention is not to show you that you can't cope, but to help you to take steps to make things better, make you better, to become a better person. To learn your lessons. Sometimes things are out of your control, they are part of the bigger divine plan. We sometimes behave as if the world is only concerned with us. It's not. It's HUGE and you are an incredibly important, yet tiny part of it all. Forgive yourself for what you think that you have or haven't done and been and set yourself free. Cut the strings that hold you in the past or in the grip of others who cannot see the truth of the wider picture. Let them be negative and bitter. You choose to move on and be the best person that you can be.

Forgiving others can be hard. Hard as it can be, as an emotional act, forgiveness frees you from the shackles of bitterness and ego. It lets you move on. It stops you from holding onto things that don't need to concern you in your here and now.

You can be happy and know that this is your life and these are your choices and thus you can grow. To live a life where you dwell on anything that has been done "to" you is a life that is shadowed by darkness. It causes you to censor your words, to ignore others and cling onto a bitterness inside that is poison to your body and soul. Your belief that you cannot ever forgive is holding you to ransom, not them, you. Only an individual person can themselves have the power to choose whether to take in another's thoughts or emotions. If the person that you are blaming for something is happily living their life whilst you are grunting at them and feeling bad then you are the loser, not them. Holding them to ransom with guilt is just as bad. You are holding yourself in a negative pattern of blame, anger and bitterness, and trying at the same time to impose on them a life of self destruction. Neither of you is learning any lessons. Be strong and be the one who walks away. Hold your spirit intact and know that you will be okay. Forgiveness, letting go, is the only way. Lighten your heart and let the light then show you the way.

Kindness to yourself generates acceptance and self love. Compassion for your own spirit will allow your wings to soar without your head being full of negative thoughts about yourself which can slow you down or stop you altogether. You have to accept you, in order to be you. You have to be kind to others in order to experience the joy of being you. We are all magical, loving souls. Once we chip off the armour of fear, we are all here to help ourselves and each other. Living in total kindness to yourself, you do not need to interact negatively with others, you get your kicks from kindness. Your reassurance from the knowledge that you are giving to others as a genuinely good person will fuel you. Your battery of goodness will be fully charged and so therefore will you.

Kindness is the currency of love, of life. People are generally pulled towards and attracted to those who express genuine kindness from their hearts. Kindness to others is your natural way of lighting you and them up. Kindness is powerful. Think of the simple everyday acts of kindness that you have received and the really kind people that you have met in your life. You remember them. They impacted you in a way that made a real difference to you. Kindness is not like a normal conversation or day to day interaction. Kindness is the most powerful nourishment in the world. It heals. It lifts the spirit. It ignites tears of laughter and joy. It touches the heart in a way that nothing else does. As simple a gesture as letting someone else go first touches the heart of them and you. It is easy, so easy to do. It doesn't have to cost anything. It is free to us all. A compliment, a kind word, a kind thought, a tiny selfless action, will all be heard, seen and felt, beyond measure.

We are all kind at heart. You know the truth of all of these words. You just have to get over the habit of the doing and self deprecation in order to bring it out fully in yourself again. Defensive people aren't kind. They attack. Strong people are kind, even with their enemies, because they know that this is the natural state. They know that they do not need to worry about themselves and therefore get defensive. They are good enough and they have the power to bring that feeling out in others.

With forgiveness and conscious kindness to yourself and others, you can turn your back on negativity and self doubt. Say goodbye to the frustration and tears caused by not feeling adequate and start learning, start living. Your lessons are the same as everyone else's. Until you start to look after yourself, let go of the past and be kind to yourself and others, you will be called here again and again.

Our natural state is love

It is natural to be you. It is not natural for you not to be you. Being someone else or hiding behind a mask or being a certain way to please others feels unnatural, uncomfortable. When you look unnatural, people don't know how to take you. They walk on eggshells around you or avoid you. People like people who feel good about themselves. Who don't have hang ups or chips on their shoulders. Your natural state is one of love. That innocent, vulnerable little person inside your heart that feels almost like pain when you feel it is actually love. You. In all of your softness and insecurity. At heart, all of us are good people. It is our negative beliefs and thoughts that fire our insecure ego which in turn causes us to harm ourselves or others. Our natural state is open, kind, loving, compassionate, and vulnerable.

When we are born we do not walk around with frowns on our faces. We play. We laugh. We smile. We are still us. If we are unsure we go for help, love, a cuddle. As we grow we somehow think that we have to be invincible and strong beyond measure and never let on how frightened we are at times. It is okay to rely on others. It is okay to need reassurance. It is okay to just need a cuddle and a few kind words.

We may have this hampered by fear at a young age as a result of difficult parentage or other less than ideal circumstances and what happens here is that we start to cover ourselves up. Beat ourselves up. Hide. Pull on the mask and start building a big strong wall. Our challenge now is to have faith that if we let go and surrender to our hearts and knock the wall down that we will be okay.

Our natural state is love. You know it. I know it. We all know it. Now we all need to be it.

Our life's mission is to be and give of ourselves

As we grow into this world those who care for us want the best for us. They teach us to set goals for achievement that will show ourselves and them that we are up to scratch. Happy. Successful. Our education systems teach us intellectual advantage. Useful lessons in making the most of our lives financially. But they also fit in with the assumption that we have to have a career or an important role to be good. As a result those who don't "have" a career or a clear role, can feel unsuccessful, less than those who do. The intellectual elite are seen as superior. A lot of people start a job and over the years realize that their heart isn't really in it and wish that they had chosen something else, usually the something else that they instinctively fancied but that their parents or society said wasn't good enough.

What job shall I go for? What kind of friends shall I have? What age shall I retire so that I can do all of the things that I want – or have a rest and stop doing and "find" myself again? Recognise yourself?

Some of the happiest people in the world are those who have very little. This is because they do not rate themselves against what they do, or how they earn money but how they feel, behave and help others. They work to live, not the other way around. The one shining difference here is that they are themselves. They accept who they are. They go through their days in their natural state, as themselves. They are on path.

All of us come to this earth with a gift. Something that once we find it, we help others beyond measure in some shape or form, maybe one person, maybe just ourselves, maybe millions. Your gift is yourself. Being you and the best of you in all of your natural loveliness is what you are here to do, what you are here to be. Not your occupation or role or lack of one. You. Some people flow through their lives and then one day they wake up with an illness, or simply a realisation that the clock has stopped for a tiny fragment of a second. Enough time for them to catch a glimpse of the realisation that there must be more to life than this. They awaken.

You are your life.

As we advance, we journey towards the truth, we live our lives in light, in enlightenment.

Until recently, when I thought of enlightenment it was about travelling to Thailand or Tibet and sitting on a mountain for a few years before the realisation of some golden truth. I now believe that it doesn't have to be like that. Meditation is without doubt a route to self knowledge, it speeds up the process. This is because it allows you to spend time with you. As you are also part of the greater question, oneness with the universe, it also allows you to spend time with source. The way that I now look at enlightenment is that it is the realisation that you are simply who you are and that this is enough. It is the realisation that you, as you are, are part of a bigger whole. It is the truth. The absolute knowing that this time that you have in this body is only temporary and that space and time means not of the earth. It is a way of being that is completely you through love. You, as the very best person that you can be. It is a state available to all, no matter who you are or where you are. All you have to do is reach into your heart, pull out you, dropping all self consciousness and fear of humiliation and present it to yourself and to the world through absolute love. Be that and enlightenment is yours.

The universe, the source, is a very powerful thing. You are it. It is it. Manifestation and healing work because you are part of the bigger whole. Spoken with positive affirmation and emotion, manifestation brings things to you and within you. If it doesn't then it is because what you are requesting you are not feeling. You are not living it with the intention of giving. When you manifest for the greater good (which includes your greater good) you step into grace. You ask to become part of the divine plan. You request to give of yourself to others so advancing your soul. Ask with a demonstration of that which you choose to create and ask it with love. Sending intention ignites and weaves a thread. Ask and it is given. Healing channels the love and power of the universe to support soul growth and beauty. Both work because they work through you and you are part of the whole.

Absolute realisation, total belief that you are your answer only truly comes when you learn the lessons. When you are living completely, practically, as love, you have no room for a negative ego. You can manage it, the ego, because it becomes what it should be, a human tool for motivation and soul growth, one of many.

Enlightenment is your total belief that you, as the best of you are enough within the bigger picture. The light bulb goes on. It all clicks into place. You become love completely. You start to realize the truth of who you really are and what all of "this" is about.

Enlightenment, the truth, is love

So the truth of this life is that we have been living an illusion. Until now most of us only realized this at the end of each life. With the dawn of the new world age we are being prepared for a new era of humanity, we are being shown the truth now. Guides and angels are working through us, as we create, to reveal the truth. Every word that is spoken from the heart is an expression of this channel. We are all part of the channel. Every creative endeavour that comes into being as we let go and reveal ourselves and our impulses is a seed in the field of advancement, of enlightenment, a revealing of the truth.

We are all love. It is at the center of all of us. Enlightenment is love because the knowing of the truth is you, and you are love. Love really is the answer.

We are all love. We are all One

Stare into the eyes of another and if you do it for long enough,
a minute or so, you will see yourself staring back.
Neale Donald Walsh

Affirmations for living my life of love

- ♥ I am myself
- ♥ I find joy by being me
- ♥ My forgiveness and kindness has opened my heart to learning and experiencing who I really am
- ♥ I am a natural expression of love
- ♥ I be me and I give of myself whenever I get the opportunity
- ♥ I am the truth
- ♥ We are all love
- ♥ We are all one

CHAPTER THREE

THE LESSONS OF LOVE

- ♥ The lesson of compassion
- ♥ The lesson of forgiveness
- ♥ The lesson of kindness
- ♥ The lesson of acceptance
- ♥ The lesson of joy

All of us struggle with the ego and the negative emotions of being human, of not letting our backgrounds and beliefs dictate who we now have to be. The lessons that the soul is here to learn and experience show us that we should let go of the negative side of human nature and become the very best of it. It is as simple as that. You will have had lives where you learnt quite a few ways of letting go of this. You will take these lessons with you into this life. You will have led lives where you embraced kindness to yourself or others. You will learn not to abandon. Not to blame. Not to walk away. Not to hurt others. Not to feel abandoned. Not to selfishly go for it all for yourself. Not to put yourself or others down. You will eventually learn that the answer is love. Once you live in love, your time here is done.

Think about the life that you lead today. Look back. How much love have you been? How much of you have you truly revealed? How much have you loved and given to yourself and others? Rate how much negative energy you have injected into yourself. How often you have compared yourself to others? How often you have put others down (including behind their back)? Have you forgiven your parents? Your playground companions? Yourself? Get a feeling of how well you are learning your lessons so far in this life, of how much love you are living, feeling and expressing?

Some of us are more advanced than others; we have learnt some lessons before. Where we haven't, we may have chosen circumstances in this life that we hope will force us to learn them. Other souls will have volunteered to help us along the way. These are the people who are with you in your life right now.

Your aim in this life is to advance your soul by being yourself and learning and living the lessons in love, within the facts of life. Let's look more deeply at what these lessons are.

Compassion. Forgiveness. Kindness. Acceptance. Joy.

The lesson of compassion

The closest some of us get to deep compassion is probably as parents. As a parent you have to put yourself second. No matter how stressed or busy you are, at that moment when your child cries in pain as they fall, you HAVE to show compassion. The world stops, your heart opens and your to do list is mentally dropped for a few seconds. Most of us are not generally compassionate. We live for ourselves. That feeling when you comfort someone, that compassion, can also be experienced when you feel slightly raw and vulnerable. It is similar. It is an opening of the heart. It is a beautiful human vulnerability. Only the strongest of people can really master compassion because you have to live with a vulnerable heart. We have to have faith that feeling vulnerable is okay and most of us don't.

If you stand in the street and open your heart you immediately feel self conscious, as if everyone is looking at you. Vulnerable. Yet if you can do this, hold no judgment and feel the love in all of the souls that you can see, then that feeling, that uplifting joy in your heart, that is the feeling of living with compassion. It is an open heartedness. A dis-engagement with the mind. You don't have to work for a charity to live with compassion. You don't have to dedicate your life to an organized religion or established way of life dictated by society. You just have to feel it. Live with feeling.

This life of yours is about being you. So compassion has to become part of being you, with feeling, with care, with open hearted concern for yourself and the world around you.

Compassion is a state of being. It is a way of life. You are asked to have compassion for yourself and those around you; to care what happens to yourself and those around you, to have concern.

Having compassion isn't simply about caring for other's misfortunes. It is also about not causing any. Be that through your words, your expressions or your actions. It is about reaching your goals in life whilst being conscious of the environment and people around you. Not upsetting others, not putting them down to make yourself feel better. Being you and using yourself at heart to live your life whilst helping others to live theirs well too.

Compassion is heart based feeling, for your circumstances, for your choices and those of others and the world around you. As a soul, you grow through a state of compassion, through living from the heart. Caring for yourself and others. Instead of always thinking about yourself and what you need and want, compassion helps you to help others and they help you in return. It is a state of softness to the self and others. Instead of living purely through the logical brain, compassion opens the heart. It touches. It is love. It is the most powerful emotion a human spirit contains. It sends waves of light and healing to you, others and the world.

All of the great saints and ascended masters were heroes of compassion. Their three dimensional lives helped to pave the way to a brighter way of life. Compassion is about looking after yourself through caring for your body. It is looking after the planet and all of the plants and animals that inhabit it. It is only taking what you need and leaving the rest for others. It is connecting with your own loving vibration and flow through your own music and song. It is being there for others and helping them out when they need it, as well as when they don't. It is noticing when you can help and doing so, without call for thanks or reciprocation.

Compassion brings an abundance of joy. It is your natural way. A feeling of heartfelt pride in yourself and others. A way of life. A connection with source. Compassion overcomes all feelings of loneliness and isolation because your focus is on love. Love of the self and love for others. Your intention is love and so love will be returned, felt.

If your focus is on the doing rather than the being, if you are thinking negatives of others, even those that you don't know, if your expectations of yourself and others are low, if you are beating yourself up, if you take as much as you can get and store it all up for a rainy day, if you can't remember the last time you were truly living from the heart, feeling emotion all around you, if you don't care about your family, your friends, your local environment, yourself, then you are not living in compassion.

If you are plodding through life, putting up with what you have been dealt, if you are crying with sadness and self doubt, if you spend your all of your leisure time shopping to look good or collecting "stuff" to make yourself feel better, if you numb the pain with TV, busyness and computer console games, you are not living in compassion.

You will come here again and again until you do.

If you want others to be happy practice compassion, if you want
to be happy practice compassion
The Dalai Lama

The lesson of forgiveness

Forgiveness releases the negative ego from the soul. It creates a space for you to manage yourself emotionally.

If your world is full of bitterness and anger at the acts that others did to you and you did to them, tit for tat, a vicious game, then the temptation for the ego is to get your own back. To come out on top. To show others that you are not what they think that you are. That you are better.

That we are hurting inside and riddled with guilt and loneliness somehow doesn't stop this rot. Power games. Control over others. Our own insecurities force us to attack, the first and commonest form of defense.

Self censorship and dancing on egg shells is also keeping others within our grip.

Let go. Be honest. Act and speak with compassion. Stop the games.

Forgive and let go.

This inner battle is like tying a huge knot inside your heart and tightening it and tightening it until you squeeze out all that you are. You are only left with the knot. You have nothing to prove in this life. You have no image that you have to portray. Your negative inner battles are only hurting yourself. You become not good enough. Not a good person. Yet it is only you that is the battle on both sides. The negative side of the human ego ties you up in knots! You have a choice. Forgive yourself for all that you haven't got and been. Start again. Jump up, dust yourself off and begin again the life that you have almost forgotten that you have. Hold no regrets. Start again.

The emotional baggage that holding onto grudges involves saps your energy and restricts your flow from the heart. If you can forgive and move on, then suddenly anything is possible. Your shackles are off. The anger and resentment dissolves. No one is holding onto you any longer. The world becomes your oyster as you experience real emotional freedom. The relief is enormous. Forgiveness then paves the way for your own path. You are able to be you and move on. You learn to reward yourself for all that you are grateful for. No more self punishment. You come to the fore. Forgiveness calms and releases you and others from having to act or please. You can rest knowing that you are in charge of your world. You can sleep. Your mind isn't constantly racing to fill in the gaps or help you to succeed because the release and freedom allow you to surrender to yourself.

Forgiveness is the fragrance that the violet sheds on the heel
that has crushed it.
Mark Twain

The lesson of kindness

Once you open your heart and let go of keeping score, kindness naturally follows. It flows. It becomes the norm.

Kindness is free. A smile. A kind word. A gift of thought. A gesture. An offer of help. Letting others go first. Thanking goodness. Acknowledging another. Blessing all that you have. Being grateful. Remembering that you are special. Watching where you walk. Planting a new spark. Giving.

Kindness is a wonderful art and a lesson that is such a pleasure to embark upon. Be as kind as you can be in your life. With a good heart, your heart, you are able to light up the world. Don't keep your compliments to yourself. Embark on a mission to give kindness to all that you meet. The feeling of specialness that the recipient will experience will brighten their day and at times will change their lives. Your giving of kindness to others tops up the happy energy in your heart. It brings reassurance to you and the world. It brings hope, optimism, positivity, love. You smile and the world really does smile with you.

Your lesson of kindness can so easily be learnt. It is conscious choice. A decision to step into and give love.

What do we live for if it is not to make life less difficult for each other?
George Elliot

The lesson of acceptance

There is one thing for sure. You are what you are. No changing it. No challenging it. Your spirit was created as you. You are it. This is it. You can choose your thoughts about it but you have to accept that you are your lot. Warts and all. All that you have got is nothing, simply a wall that covers up your truth, your soul. Tall, small, fat, thin, pink, white, black, brown. You are you. Accept it. Because until you do, you will never be you. You will come here life after life again and again trying to be someone that you are not.

Only you think that what you are is not a lot. You think that you should be this or that. You are you. Sorry, but that's that. Accept it. Be it. The minute that you do the relief will enfold you. We must all accept that we have come to this earth as who we are to explore.

It is the same for others around you too. They will start to accept who they are when you do. When you let that mask go and let down your guard to reveal who you really are, they will drop theirs too. They will feel the freedom of being themselves. Acceptance is like relief bottled and wrapped in a huge chocolate bar. Relief beyond measure. You can let go. Be who you are.

Choose to take the first step right here and simply accept that where you are in your life is where you are meant to be Everything happens for a reason. You may not be able to fathom it now but one day you will. You will look back and see how ingenious the grand plan really is. Mechanical grace, all flexibl

and all set up for you to be you. You'll learn your lessons when you choose to and be totally supported. By accepting what is, you can release negative emotion and move forward.

For me this has been one of the hardest lessons so far. The self consciousness of not really accepting myself for who I am. The embarrassment of being me. I can remember having to stand up to do reading in primary school. I was probably about eight. I was not a good reader and had some difficulty in reading fluidly. At eight you don't easily accept that it is okay to be like this, to be and accept who you are. You are surrounded by people who are suddenly better than you. To be you means stuttering and sounding stupid. All eyes are upon you and your bright red cheeks make you ask for the ground to open up and swallow you whole! I can remember, again as a child, being really embarrassed when asked my name, when I actually spoke the words of my name, I was so embarrassed. How ridiculous!

Not accepting myself has made me control. If like me you have struggled with this one you have to accept that you are simply who you are and not compare yourself to others. Accept that you don't always have to have all of the answers and be good at everything. It is okay to be different. You don't have to censor yourself all of the time and control your being and acting. You can be brave and have the courage to strike out on your own to be who you truly are.

Don't go where the path may lead, go instead where there is no path and leave a trail.
Ralph Waldo Emerson

Yes, you are asked to be the best of who you are but only you have the choice of how you express it. That surrender to yourself can feel totally bizarre. It means believing that you are your star. You are your answer. You are who you are. But my goodness what a relief.

You are wonderful, you are unique, you are special, you are light, you are love.

And that is enough.

The lesson of joy

Honestly, for me this has been the hardest idea to get my heart around. I am quite a serious soul so having fun all of the time doesn't really feel like me. I have struggled to identify my own joy. I used to watch others joking about at school and wonder what everyone was laughing about! Was I the only one who didn't get it or was everyone thinking the same and just pretending that they got it? Had my laughter light been extinguished by the trials of my childhood? Was I condemned to seriousness and sadness for the rest of my life? What is this fun all about?

Wisdom through age is a marvellous thing. I now accept my loving seriousness, in fact I laugh at it!

I recently heard "super coach" Michael Neil in a seminar and he said something that really rang true for me on this subject. During the seminar he asked a willing volunteer to come up in front of the audience and get coached live with him. Towards the end of the demonstration he asked them what their life would be like, feel like, look like if they were always having fun, and just left it with them. Interesting isn't it. He said "What would all fun be like for you? Spend your doing as being focused upon having fun".

He is of course right. When you are really being you, you let go and when you let go, you are having fun. This doesn't mean that you spend your whole time rolling around on the floor laughing, although that sounds great too! In England, where I live, the word fun is quite narrow in its general meaning, it's all about laughter. But fun in America can be just fun. Doing something that you enjoy, reading something interesting, is fun.

In other words just doing something that you really enjoy, doing it in a way that is really in line with who you are, is fun. This is, to my way of thinking, a much better and broader definition.

For me then fun is feeling love and warmth. It is reading a touching word or pulling out an angel card. It is food shopping and staring excitedly into other's trolleys working out what kind of meal they will be eating for dinner and who they are and what they like. It is lying in bed with my morning coffee. Sipping a lovely glass of wine in front of the fire. Dancing in the kitchen with my little girl. A cuddle. A marshmallow!

Joy is actually following your own bright star – yes – once again in stereo – who you are. Follow what you love and you will feel good. You will be yourself. Ask yourself what you would love to be doing right now and go and do it, right now.

If you feel anxious or timid or your intuition tells you that something is wrong then it probably is. Step away and re-center yourself, become more conscious. Make the choice that needs to be made and do more of what you enjoy. Joy opens the gateway to really being the best of who you are. No room for negativity. Your mission is to have joy whilst you are here. How can you have joy when you are not enjoying life. You'll close down.

Do what makes you happy in a way that feels good and you'll enjoy being you and getting to know and remembering who you are.

Affirmations for living my life of love

- ♥ I care for myself and the world around me
- ♥ I love being me
- ♥ I forgive and let go
- ♥ I am calm and free to be myself
- ♥ I bless all that I have, all that I see and all that I meet
- ♥ I am wonderful just as I am
- ♥ I fill my time doing the things that I love
- ♥ I have fun being me

To advance your soul the lessons of love have to be applied to
Loving yourself
Loving others
Living love in life

CHAPTER FOUR

LOVING YOURSELF

You have incarnated again and again but with the challenge of not remembering that you have done so. You will naturally bring with you the lessons that you have already learnt but, if you want to reach enlightenment and advance your soul in this incarnation, you will have to learn the lesson of loving yourself.

Our higher dimensional reality, as a soul, is amazing. It is home. When people "die" before you, you don't lose them, you join them again at the end of this life. You cannot imagine the loving arms that will enfold you when you leave the earth plane and experience you again. We do not need to be afraid. Death is actually life once again. Our souls will be back in the safe hands of our soul group and source until we are ready to face this three dimensional challenge once again. If we can love ourselves whilst we are here in the way that we do when we are there, then we will have an earthly experience beyond measure. We will get the chance to be and give the best of everything, manifested. What an opportunity!

So you do not need to be afraid that if you die you will be leaving everything behind. Our loved ones that have been here in the world with us are still with us now. In fact in some senses they are more with us now than they were when they were living their most recent three dimensional life. Before my wonderful grandmother died I hardly ever saw her. She was at one end of the country and I was at the other. Now I can speak to her and feel her whenever I like. I feel closer to her now then when she was "alive". The reassurance then is that she is still alive. She is just vibrating at a different frequency, one that mediums can feel and communicate with and some can actually see. Every soul who has been here is still around, you just have to call to them and feel them in your heart and they are there. My daughter closes her eyes and has conversations with Gran. She can always tell me what she is eating! My grandmother loved to eat when she was here so why would she be any different when my daughter sees her in her heart's eye now?

After she had died I spoke with a medium who got her straight away. On the day of her funeral, I had visited her in the funeral home. I had taken a tiny posy of flowers, which I had placed in her hands. The medium told me this and he had no idea that I had done that. The medium even said that they were white and yellow – and they had been! You cannot argue with that. It is a fact. She is still here.

Both my grandmothers died in the last few years and I can now feel them both. They have conversations with me in my energy. When we leave here we don't leave. We just go home – back to our natural vibration. This is what will happen to you when you go too.

Self love is the gateway to the enlightened soul. You have to love you. If awakening is the doorframe, then love is the door and you, my friend, are love, you are also what is on the other side because love is all there is. Loving yourself is the first step to advancement.

Your journey so far

Let's start by having a look at your journey in this life so far. In order to progress, you have to first look at where you are and what loving you involves. Before we begin, recognize that as a soul you have really come far. To be reading these words means that you are ready and open to really being and experiencing all that you are. This exercise is one of loving you. So take the first step towards that by being kind to yourself.

Take a pencil and ask yourself by ticking or crossing these

questions if you have so far been truly loving you...

- ❤ Do you truly believe in yourself?
- ❤ Do you feel that you can be you in the things that you do?
- ❤ Do you always tell yourself positive things about yourself?
- ❤ Do you look after yourself?
- ❤ Do you take time out to look after you?
- ❤ Do you feel comfortable with your body, especially when around others?
- ❤ Do you feel healthy?
- ❤ Are you free from disease?
- ❤ Do you happily share your thoughts and opinions?
- ❤ Do you always know that your opinion of yourself is what really matters?
- ❤ Do you always show you?
- ❤ Do you give yourself enough sleep?
- ❤ Do you care for your body?
- ❤ Do you allow yourself to do what you love?
- ❤ Do you always show yourself kindness?
- ❤ Do you truly accept who you are?
- ❤ Do you let go of the past?
- ❤ Do you forgive you?
- ❤ Do you hold onto your heart and enjoy the view?

I could go on and on, but I think that you get the gist. Are you looking after yourself and believing and feeling that it is okay to simply be you?

Self harm is the doorway to darkness and I am not just talking about physical harm or neglect. If you answered no to any of the questions above then your soul has work to do. You have to start looking after yourself, loving yourself.

The key question here is do you genuinely love being you. Does being you fill your heart with warmth? If you do and none of this is news to you then fantastic – go to the next chapter and look to learn something new. If the answer is no then stay here and let's look more closely at loving you.

Opening the doorway to you

Start by thinking, feeling and writing down all of the wonderful things that you love about being you. Don't be modest. This list is for you. Do you love your hair, your attitude, your job, your life? What do you love about the things on your list? What makes you truly grateful for being you? What wouldn't you change about yourself? What are the truly beautiful attributes of your soul? Fill a page with all of the wonders of you.

Your ego is screaming NO! Be modest. Don't do it!

Even if you feel you can't write it or choose not to at this moment, hold this book in your hands, close your eyes and feel the appreciation of you, send enormous blessings to yourself. Fill your heart with love. Now write it! Stop avoiding yourself, open yourself to love.

Loving yourself is the first step towards advancement. You will always find it difficult to master the lessons of compassion, forgiveness, kindness, acceptance and joy if you don't reflect these things back to yourself.

All the things that I love about being me...

Even more things that I love about being me (come on go for it!)...

What makes us not love ourselves?

To open the doorway we need to understand ourselves better by looking at what stops us from loving ourselves and what we can do about it.

Self defeating behavior, switching off, logging off from life, blaming others for your pain and low energy are all giving away your power and control in your life. We all know people with chips on their shoulders, the question is how big is yours?

Most people think that life happens to them.

The problem with this is that they give away all of their power. If you blame your background, your parents, your lack of money, your friends, people and circumstances that have hurt you, if you blame them for where you are in your life and how you feel, then you are giving away all of your power and control to them. This makes you feel out of control and tells you that you are not good enough. "None of this is my fault". The thing is that we do know inside that we could have taken back control at any time. It's just been easier not to. If we accept responsibility at any given moment, then we will expose ourselves. We are nowhere near ready, we are not good enough. And so blaming others for the state of our lives allows us to feel that we have done nothing wrong. It somehow shows us that we are okay and the rest of the world is not. We can continue to hide.

The problem is that it feels dreadful. We build up walls and masks to hide ourselves from the world because we know that we are not good enough, that we could have taken back control but that we didn't. We become defensive. We moan. We become negative. We throw out sarcastic comments to put others down, thinking that we will then look and feel better. We don't. We feel a bitter regret that eats away at our health and well being and confirms that yes, we are not good enough. Others withdraw from us and we congregate with those we feel superior to or other bitter souls who have lost their way. Like them, we spend our lives showing one thing and then privately beating ourselves up to oblivion. Occasionally we press self destruct, over eat, lash out, drink. We numb the pain with negative thoughts and comparisons. Other times we lead a life of quiet desperation.

We all have an element of this within us. Some more than others. We also all have the choice to do something about it. We can continue to choose to let life control us and continue to feel dreadful, or we can be defiant in love and say "no, from now on I am choosing to live my life in love."

You dictate your reactions to life. You tell yourself that you are good enough. Take the bull by the horns and start truly living. Take responsibility for who you are and choose to be positive and kind to yourself and others. Choose your eyes to be windows of love. See the best in life, choose to see the best in others. Choose to see and be the best in yourself.

Stop the rot. Only you can do it. Only you have the power to uncover and be brave and bring out the best in you. Take back control. Stand firm in your power, your choice. Use forgiveness, compassion, acceptance and kindness to release yourself from the trap.

Your lessons of self love

You hold all of the tools to feeling amazing, to feeling loved, to opening the door to your own advancement. Learn the lessons and apply them to yourself. Okay, here we go...

- Compassion: care about yourself and your health and happiness. Open to and follow your feelings.
- Forgiveness: forgive yourself for the past and your reactions to the hurts and actions of others.
- Kindness: choose positivity and give yourself only kind words and kind treatment.
- Acceptance: lift the negativity so that you can express you,

your heart. Stand in your truth and accept who you are.

- Joy: follow who you are, your joy. Be who you are. Enjoy being you.

I love myself with compassion

Treat yourself as you would like to be treated by others. We are often our own worst enemies. We beat ourselves up. We negatively compare who we are with others. We carry on regardless by numbing our consciousness, never listening to ourselves, only the drum of the busyness, the constant noise of the TV, the radio, the doing doing doing. You are in there under all of this hiding. Lift yourself out of it. Stop, be still, listen to your inner voice. Cry the tears of the past and the ones of joy at the discovery that little old you, lovely you, that little boy or girl is there under it all, still intact and ready to start a new dawn.

Give yourself a conscious health and heart check. Care for yourself by noting any physical parts of your body that need some TLC and take care of it. If you are tearful or sad, ask yourself what you are mourning, who are you leaving behind, what hurts are you still recovering from and go and get what you need to care for your heart and soul. Go and seek help if you need to or start a journal or a letter to tell yourself and express all that you have held back.

How happy are you? What's going well in your life? What are you surprised at? What would you like to change? What are you feeling? What do you regret? Consciously evaluate your heart and with compassion change the habit of logical, realistic living. When life takes over gently remind yourself to feel again. Do a quick feel check to remind yourself to love living and enjoy and care for who you are.

We bury our feelings. We are encouraged not to be emotional, not to cry, not to be soft. But you are soft! You are an emotional being! Care for the love in you, have compassion for your own being. Listen to your feelings and express them.

When my parents divorced, as a child my feeling and pain was beyond measure. I tried and tried to bury and deny, but occasionally the fizzy lemonade bottle would be shaken and the torrent of love would be expressed. The pain would flow out of me. The compassion for myself would take over. I was a child. It was natural. It still is, even for adults, but others have told us that it is childish to behave this way. It's not, it's who you are! My instinct, just as yours is, is to be compassionate to myself. We are all the tiny child within us. We are all vulnerable and made of pure love. Don't deny your feelings, feel them, express them. Smile through your tears. The healing that your self care will have will be without bounds. Tend your wounds lovingly. It's okay to be hurt. It's okay to be afraid. Love the softness within you. It will provide you with enormous strength through self love.

Follow your feelings and trust your heart. It will lead you further towards love. Care for you with positive grace. You are your own light, so you have to take care of that light, take care of yourself.

Make a list of the things that you are going to change or be, the things that show your care for yourself and your compassion for who you are. Will you give yourself a break? Slow down and listen to your heart more often? Will you wake up each morning and recount all of the wonderful feelings and excitement that you have in your heart? Will you stop making head lists and start making heart ones? Will you follow your heart and intuition? Will you care for your body with compassion? What will you do? Our intentions are strengthened enormously when we write them down, so do it. Write them here, right now and actively love yourself with compassion.

I will love myself with compassion by...

-
-

-
-
-
-
-
-

I love myself with forgiveness

We have all done things that we are not proud of. Sometimes, sarcastic and unkind words leave our lips without us even registering. Our own insecurities and their influence on our conscious and sub conscious behaviors are very powerful. Forgiveness of these actions, thoughts and behaviors will set you free so that you are not bound by your insecurities into a powerless life. You can shake off your wrong doings and regrets and set yourself free. If you spend any time dwelling on your past and letting your regrets dictate your now, then you are holding yourself a prisoner. You can't change the past, so say sorry if you can to the others, say sorry to yourself for your actions or lack of them, and then move on.

Holding ourselves in chains gets us nowhere. We will achieve and learn nothing. By forgiving you'll strengthen your spirit. Know that you cannot achieve perfection by holding yourself back. Aim for perfection by being active and learning from your mistakes and lessons. Let the past go.

Whether you think that you have or haven't done enough, whether you have harmed another, or yourself, whatever you have or haven't done, know that it is the past and redeem yourself from a life of regret.

Your greatest gift to the world is yourself. How can the world truly receive that gift if you don't release it from whatever has or hasn't happened, where it remains shackled by the grief of guilt.

Forgive yourself for the past and your reactions to the hurts and actions of others.

If you are still holding onto anger and resentment towards others, then know that this is hurting yourself more than you know. They might have moved on, maybe they haven't. But by holding them angrily in your heart, you are suffocating your own love, your own light. You are letting the shadow of yourself and others dampen your happiness, your spirit. Your mission here is to be you. You have the opportunity to glow. Choose to forgive.

Write it down now.

I choose to love myself with forgiveness by letting go of these regrets and resentments...

-
-
-
-
-
-
-
-

I love myself with kindness

One of the kindest things that you can do in extreme adversity or when negative, harmful energy comes in to your aura, is to cocoon your soul. Not hiding, but protecting, cocooning. Victims of any kind of harm, be it emotional or physical, know this. It is a natural self protection mechanism. It is your soul choosing to not let the environment attack and infect who you are and instead to hibernate and protect your beautiful spirit from any infection.

When you are hurting and life strikes a painful blow, cocooning feels like you are enveloping your heart. It is a going within, not to avoid the situation or to ignore it but simply to rest inside your shell, whilst at the same time knowing that you are okay. You are a good, vulnerable spirit, and you seek counsel with yourself in your own heart. It's like consciously wrapping your inner beauty in pink candy floss to buffer the ride. I cocooned as a child.

Barry Manilow (my favorite of favorites!) sings a beautiful song which he names "I made it through the rain". I love this song. It describes cocooning and how I feel, having come through the shadows of my own hurts; "I kept myself protected" and "Kept my point of view" and "Found myself respected by the others who got rained on too and made it through"...and so can you.

Cocooning has been so powerful for me. It is a clear demonstration and guide of how to be totally kind to yourself, either in or following adversity. By protecting your love and your vulnerable heart, they stay intact, growing in strength. By protecting your vulnerability, you choose to be kind to your heart by not destroying it. This is what kindness to yourself is. It is the opposite of self destruction.

Know that you are capable of getting through anything that life throws at you. Protect and cocoon the love and kind heart that you hold within you. Gain strength as your life unfolds, despite its challenges. Love yourself through kindness by chasing away the fears in your head and your heart and live your life with an open grace.

Choose to give yourself only kindness. Choose to be positive about who you are and devote your inner talk to building up your inner strength by using kind words and thoughts about yourself and your life. Stop being so hard on yourself. Celebrate all that you have and are achieving. Know that the kindness inside you is a gift to your soul. A gateway to you.

I choose to love myself with kindness by...

-
-
-
-
-
-
-
-

I love myself with acceptance

Stand in your truth and accept who you are. You can choose to change it but, by taking on the roles, behaviors and actions of others as your own, you are only dampening your light and increasing your belief that you are not good enough. Comparing yourself to others, living as others live, will never make you happy. Let them be them and you be you. You are good enough. Earlier I asked you to write down everything you love yourself for. Read your list again now. Only you think that you are not good enough. You perceive that you are seen as inadequate but actually you will be touched and happily amazed at how wonderful those around you think that you are. Make a list here of all the reasons that you are good enough.

I have shown that I am good enough by...

-
-
-
-
-
-
-
-

What have you done to help, to give, to be kind? What have you achieved in your life? If you are choosing to ignore the good within you, know that you are choosing to be the victim and give away your power. Your neediness through negative attention is holding back your soul. You are the one with the chip on your shoulder by your own choice. No one else's.

Stand in your strength, your goodness, your good enough-ness and accept yourself. Feel the relief of it. You don't have to try any more. You just have to be. You don't have to do and become all of the "shoulds" that are surrounding you and sapping your energy and your time. You, as you are, is all that matters. You are good enough! Say it to yourself. "I am good enough". Know it, breathe it, repeat it to yourself when you doubt yourself or you feel self consciousness creeping in.

If you struggle to believe it, then know that you are choosing to, no one else. Leave modesty at the gates and bask in your own goodness for a second. Then go and be yourself. Stand in your truth. Let the world bathe in you.

By walking around pleasing everyone and never saying no, you are not accepting yourself because you are doing these things to look good in the eyes of others. Be your own approval system. Judge yourself against yourself in kindness, acceptance and forgiveness. Take care of you first.

Sometimes when we reflect on being ourselves we can become embarrassed. This is because of those "shoulds" again. I have had moments in my life when I have cried and screamed and cried again – it's embarrassing. It's also me. I can't hold in emotion and so it just expresses itself whenever I try to hold it in. I am an emotional, very emotional, sensitive soul. This isn't a bad thing. I sometimes thought it was when perhaps I became emotional and couldn't control it. As I have grown older and wiser, I have learnt that I need to stand in my truth and express it. When I can consciously do this – and this is what true acceptance takes, true consciousness – then the top doesn't fly off the fizzy lemonade

bottle, not apart from when it does naturally because you are genuinely expressing something. The desire to please and be liked is there for all of us. Learn the lesson. Accept who you are and enjoy standing in yourself. You are great. Let the world know it.

Accept you, like yourself for who you are and let that be enough.

I love myself with joy

The "shoulds" creep into our lives without us even noticing. I should be doing this. I shouldn't be doing that. Yes we all need to have a roof over our heads as do those who depend on us. We need to eat. We need to keep warm. But beyond those needs what we then need to be and feel is completely content. The problem is that for most of us we have let society and the views and rules of our communities, families, friends and countries dictate how we behave. We have moulded ourselves and our lives to fit the should of what we are doing, at our age, in our environment. Most of us feel lost and unhappy with how we spend our time. Our perception that there is not enough of what we might need makes us strive and hoard until perhaps we reach the point where we have all of this "stuff" which we don't know what to do with and very little happiness in our hearts.

When you were a child you played. You chose what you played with. You had your favorite toys, the one or two that you preferred playing with the most. You liked them because you found joy when you played with them. You were interested, involved, lost in your joyful doing.

As adults we don't play anymore. We should. Playing isn't only reserved for the under 16's and over 60's! You don't have to change your job or your role. Five minutes of pure fun a day is a great start and not a selfish one but a loving one. Giving joy to your soul. Do what you'd love to be doing right now. Only you put the wall up that says that you can't. You might need to do only a small amount of it at first so that you make the transition physically and financially. As you give yourself more joy you might have to forgo some of your "stuff" and "shoulds" in order to keep doing it. When you truly start following what you love you won't care so much for all of the "stuff". You will be being yourself, experiencing your joy and it doesn't get any better than that. The route? Start being brave, being conscious and start enjoying all of the many aspects of this three dimensional life. Joy to you might be working, it might be singing, playing with your children, baking, running, swimming, sharing a joke, writing a poem, fixing an engine. Being.

There is more to life than your work. Remember that. You can experience your joy in every conscious moment. Bottle your moments of magic. Follow your instincts. Let go and let god. Follow your bliss, your inner joy and the world will truly begin to receive the real you. You will leave the world of numbing and hiding behind and explore with wide childlike eyes and a peaceful, excited heart, the joy of being you. Do what you feel like doing. Look for the wonder in things. Remember who you really are.

I choose to love myself with joy by...

-
-
-
-
-
-
-
-

Self love & forgiveness gives birth to unconditional love.

Affirmations for living my life of love

- ♥ I am made of pure love
- ♥ When I am unsure I know that I hold all of the answers
- ♥ I choose to take care of me
- ♥ I am comfortable with myself
- ♥ I am amazing
- ♥ I am good enough
- ♥ I am happy
- ♥ I create the love in my heart
- ♥ I choose to experience joy in every moment

CHAPTER FIVE

LOVING OTHERS

Spread love everywhere you go. Let no one ever come to you
without leaving happier.
Mother Teresa

As part of writing this book I went along to share some of it with
a local primary school. The children there were between the ages
of 4 and 11. We spent half an hour writing a book on kindness
together. The ideas and love that they shared with me and each
other were lovingly inspiring, and we hoped a real symbol of
hope to our humanity. Let me share with you their beautiful
words in hope that they will warm up the world and help it to
grow in kindness.

Our School's Book of Kindness

Kindness is being nice, being fair, sharing and friendship.

When I am kind to others I feel proud, really happy, excited,
excellent, outstanding and joyful!

When someone is kind to me I feel happy, joyful, astounding
and excellent.

To be kind to myself I tell myself that I have nice hair, I give
myself a pat on the back, I feed myself well, I give myself a treat
(like a sweet!).

I show kindness to myself by being brave enough to try
something new because then you feel like you have accomplished
something important.

I can be kind to others by being generous, by smiling, by
helping my Mummy at home, by being thoughtful, by being

grateful.

Others are kind to me when they play with me, when they are good to me, when they help me up when I fall over.

When I am unkind I feel sad, ashamed, heartbroken and annoyed.

When I typed the children's words into the manuscript I thought that they looked a little boring. They were quotations after all. And so to accentuate them I centered them... look again now.

Our School's Book of Kindness
Kindness is being nice, being fair, sharing and friendship.
When I am kind to others I feel proud, really happy, excited, excellent, outstanding and joyful!
When someone is kind to me I feel happy, joyful, astounding and excellent.
To be kind to myself I tell myself that I have nice hair, I give myself a pat on the back, I feed myself well, I give myself a treat (like a sweet!).
I show kindness to myself by being brave enough to try something new because then you feel like you have accomplished something important.
I can be kind to others by being generous, by smiling, by helping my Mummy at home, by being thoughtful, by being grateful.
Others are kind to me when they play with me, when they are good to me, when they help me up when I fall over.
When I am unkind I feel sad, ashamed, heartbroken and annoyed.

Now if you are looking for the proof that love is all that is real in this life and that a great power connects us, there it is. We wanted the words to be "a real symbol of hope to our humanity". Recognize the symbol?

When I did this I burst into tears. It's simply amazing. Each child said the right things at the right time in the right sequence for us. All divinely controlled and delivered. Grace speaking through us.

Look at the heart running behind their words! Source, love and strength are with us at every moment and in every message. I feel touched beyond measure by this demonstration for the world. Become the light. Let the children's words warm up and ignite your soul. Thank you, universe, for being with us that day, for demonstrating such love, oneness, and support to the world through this teaching.

Your lessons of loving others

Acceptance, love and understanding illustrate and bring about the power of the heart. When you apply the lessons of compassion, forgiveness, kindness, acceptance and joy to others you light up their souls and help them to see the beauty in who they are and what is all around them. Not only that, but you light up your own soul too.

When you love others you are loving yourself.

Most of my children are asleep and so I have sent you down there to wake them up and show them who they really are, by showing them who you really are.
Neale Donald Walsh

It feels so much better to love others. To show them the best of who they are by being the best of who you are. Your motor will become charged up with happiness. The inner cycle of your beliefs will give you confidence in who you are by providing the evidence that you are a great person, that you are good enough. My mother gave me a great example of this the other week. She was driving along a motorway on her way to see us. A lorry in the slow lane moved into her way rather quickly. She could have sworn and waved her first and got cross, but instead she graciously let him in with love and got a thank you and a warm heart in return. Much better than a scowl and a bad mood!

I love others with compassion

Care. Care about those around you, not just about yourself. Open your heart and your world to others. Let them in. Don't hide or hold down your feelings. Aim to warm someone else up by thinking of others as often as you can. Many people have this terrible belief – give someone an inch and they will take a mile. For some perhaps this is true, but that is because from the space that they are coming from they cannot see love, only anger and fear, a fear that they must hold onto everything, in case there isn't enough. Survival of the fittest.

Know that there is enough. Think and care and feel for others. Put yourself in their shoes. Let go of your doing mind and share what you are feeling with someone else. When you are doing something for someone, ask yourself if you are really doing it for them or for yourself? Self gratification through giving and gifting isn't compassion. Compassionate people care because they care, not because they want to be seen to be generous or a good person. A truly compassionate person does not need to have their grace acknowledged by others, it doesn't even cross their minds, their focus is on the other, and not upon themselves.

Believe in the abilities of others. Boost them. Aim to ignite their soul. Help them to find their way. Light up their path with your instinctive wisdom and care. Think about what others need. Engineer their environment to make it just right for them. Anticipate their wants. Imagine what would bring them joy and give it to them.

Not caring is not loving. You will come here again and again and be presented with something to care about, someone to care for with an open heart. From a cat to a person! Our natural state is love. Therefore if you are not loving others with compassion, then you will not be being yourself. This will stick to you like uncomfortable glue. You will feel shame, anger, regret. Turn around full circle and scoop up all that you love in your wide loving arms and apply deep care. When you care for others you care for yourself. We are all one. We are all love. You gain that which you are. So if you give love to others, you will receive love into yourself.

This life of ours is a cycle: what we give, we receive. Imagine then how wonderful if we loved with compassion and were loved with compassion right back. That is the truth of it. The flow from within between all creatures. One heart. One love.

Care about others with compassion and feel love flow.

I love others with forgiveness

Okay this is a big one for most of us. Remember that your lessons are to be remembered. You can forgive. You have no room for forgiveness in other dimensions. You know that you do not need to hold on to anyone or anything. You see only the truth. The love. Fear is what makes us unforgiving. If you spend your energy looking at how others treat you and make that your judgeometer of yourself, then you will be constantly disappointed because you cannot control or always understand the ways that others show or don't show that they love you, that they care or that they don't care. Rather than does this person love me, can I feel and see that demonstration, therefore I am loved and lovable, you could make it, what am I doing to show this person that I love them? What am I doing or not doing to show that they are loved and that they are lovable. This is tough for some relationships and people because it is the opposite of what we are used to. We are taught by our parents that when they are pleased with us then we are loved. Love is seen by us as conditional. They might love us anyway – unconditionally – but what they really show, what we see, is that when we are good we are loved. And so we spend our adult lives trying to be good to others in order for them to love us. We look for signs of that love. If we don't see the signs, then we get cross and anxious. We can't understand why being good isn't working – we can't feel the reassurance of love being returned.

Until we learn to forgive others for not living up to our own expectations, we will always be caught in this trap of searching and then experiencing heartache when we don't find what we want to find. People are not there just for you. You are there just for you. You can give and forgive and accept and bring joy and those gifts go way beyond today's modern life experience. That is to pour out my heart in love and pain to forgive the one person who, without knowing it, had taught me one of the grandest lessons of this life of ours. To forgive is to spend a life free. To hold on to the hurt and resentment is to chain ourselves and each other to a life of obligation and emotional slavery.

Lessons in Forgiveness

Forgiveness at a deep level can prove very hard. Most of us need to forgive our parents, family, carers, ex partners or even our own children for what they did or didn't do for us. Some of us were physically and sexually abused. Some of us were abandoned. These wounds run deep within us and to live in love they need to be healed.

In my life I thought that I had dealt with my childhood wounds in therapy when I was in my early thirties, until after 4 years of IBS in my late 30's I realised that I was still holding resentment towards both of my parents.

My Mom and Dad divorced when I was three years old. My brother and I lived with our mother and saw our father every other weekend. We were challenged with poverty and stigma as were most single parent families and violence entered our home when I was eight years old for a while. Our father remarried and started a new family and although we still saw him we were suddenly outside of his main family unit. When I was fifteen my mother began spending six months of the year in New Zealand. She enjoyed her life and began exploring. She had spent many years working hard often with multiple jobs. And so as I was growing up I spent most of my time at home alone or at work, to fill time outside of school.

Resentment will manifest in the body at some point in our lives and to truly love we have to deal with it.

I know how hard forgiveness at this level can be and I want to share a process with you to help you to forgive and move on from your hurts.

Firstly remember this, you agreed to all of your life circumstances before you began this life to set you on course to learn your lessons. In other words you at a soul level agreed to all of the hurts in your life. What this means is that the souls that hurt you or set up circumstances and environments that hurt you agreed to take those actions to support you. Not only this but just as you are made of pure love, so are they.

We tend to hang on to these deep resentments and allow ourselves to wallow in them. However, once you realize the truth of this life of ours, you can suddenly comprehend that these people that you blame, actually gave you a blessing. They gave you a gift. This acceptance and the counting of these blessings allows you to reframe your experiences and set yourself and them free. As Jesus said "the truth will set you free".

The behaviour of others that you hold as resentment were divinely orchestrated to allow you to learn your lessons and live centred in love. Whether it was through violence, a broken marriage or early death. If you take each hurt and each person and identify the lesson that they gave to you, you will find that you begin to thank them instead of curse them.

Take each person who you feel resentful towards and write down the lessons that they supported you with. Here's one of mine:

Dear Mom and Dad, thank you for your blessings. This list is felt with joy, not blame. I thank you from the depths of my soul for your loving actions that have supported me in learning the following lessons:

- ✔ The world is a small place
- ✔ There is more to life than work
- ✔ Leisure and adventure bring joy
- ✔ I am a loving mother
- ✔ I am independent

- ✔ Working hard brings great rewards
- ✔ Make the most of life
- ✔ Life gets better as you get older
- ✔ Separation drives resilience and determination to succeed in life
- ✔ I grow beyond my pain
- ✔ There is a wider truth spiritually
- ✔ Don't abandon others, enjoy relationships
- ✔ Build a family unit
- ✔ Family bonds are special
- ✔ I can achieve anything if I put my heart and mind into it
- ✔ Listening and supporting brings out the best in others
- ✔ I have business abilities
- ✔ I can parent a softer way
- ✔ Think of others and not just your own needs and wants
- ✔ I can cut cords
- ✔ Pain can reveal a loving heart
- ✔ It is ok to depend upon others
- ✔ Treat those you love equally

This is not an exercise of blame. It is an exercise of thanks. Without these lessons that they both lovingly agreed to give me I would not be as broad minded about the world. I would not really focus on my own family unit of my husband and daughter with such determination. I would not be decisive enough to think that I can run my own business. I may not have known that my heart was wide enough to write this guide for you.

The same applies to your Mom, Dad, Foster parents, ex Wife, ex Husband, Family, ex friends etc. Everything is set up to support you to live this life centred in love so be thankful for every pain and allow yourself to be joyous about all of your experiences.

Take pen to paper and begin your lists. Do it now and feel the joy and happiness that replaces the resentment.

Focus on one blessing, one lesson given each day. Take each one in turn and reflect on it.

Give thanks in your heart for all of the gifts that it has allowed you to be and bring. It may take a month or so to get through your list but what a relief for you and for them.

You have set your soul free.

Dear _____, thank you for your blessings. This list is felt with joy, not blame. I thank you from the depths of my soul for your loving actions that have supported me in learning the following lessons;

- ✔
- ✔
- ✔
- ✔
- ✔
- ✔
- ✔
- ✔
- ✔
- ✔
- ✔
- ✔
- ✔
- ✔
- ✔
- ✔
- ✔
- ✔
- ✔
- ✔
- ✔

making others unhappy. Which one do you choose? Sometimes we can say things in the heat of the moment and then it's too late. The only way out is to say sorry and learn not to do it again. But being unkind is a way of being that can easily be avoided. We simply have to be conscious of other people's feelings and make them the priority with compassion, rather than letting our own insecurities dictate negative actions. If you have children then you will know how cruel some children can be. Children lie and put others down to make themselves look better – as do adults! Think about the bullies and think about the children who pick on others to make themselves feel better. Perhaps you know about this from your own playground experiences. Here hearts jostle for attention, for the first tastes of power, power over others. A few children discover the inner power that control over others brings. The young ego grabs hold of its followers and commences its fight for supremacy in the battle for hearts and the limelight.

Those children with a strong soul disposition seem to stand outside of the fray. They have learnt this lesson before. Their young minds unconsciously resist and their instincts keep them away. As a result, their inner hearts remain pure. They continue to see the wonder in beauty. They remain open and giving to those on their wavelength. All whilst the others march forth as before, their souls here to learn the same lessons once more.

If you have children, encourage them to always be kind. Talk to them about the reasons why other children might be unkind. It is always the insecure and weak hearted who choose to walk the path of soul destruction through unkindness both in childhood and adulthood. Teach yourself and your children not to gossip, not to talk about others behind their backs, not to lie, not to whisper so that others think that they are being left out and not loved, not to exclude certain children or other adults from play and social experience, just because they are slightly different, or quieter than others. Choosing to be kind is just that. A choice. Learn the lesson of giving kindness to others and experience the wonder of a powerful heart, centered in love.

Kindness reigns all over the world. Make it a huge part of yours.

Here is a selection of inspiring stories of kindness from all over our world...

Maureen, South Island New Zealand

When I moved down here to the South Island, the temperature dropped well below minus and we had snow and guess what no firewood for heating! I went into town to the information center to see if they knew anybody who could deliver a load that day. Well one of the customers (on a bike) and about 75yrs old, told me to drive around to her house and load up my boot with her firewood. The next thing a lady from the back came out and made me the same offer of wood from her place. As I had never met any of these people and was a complete stranger, I found the whole thing very moving. Needless to say I got some firewood and have had a fire going ever since.

Sam, Australia

When we arrived in Sydney to live here we knew nobody! Despite this we had three Christmas invites from people we had never met before, we were given a fridge and a bed, again from people we had only just met, wonderful random acts of kindness.

Here are some lovely examples from England where I live...

Sophie, England

A stranger just stopped me on the street to return the £5 I had dropped. It made my day. Later there were no trolleys at the supermarket and I saw someone fetch one of the smaller ones for an elderly lady from the other side of the car park.

Lisa, England

I was in a toddler group with my son and he was (and still is unfortunately) going through the hitting phase. He hit a little crawling baby who was interested in the toy he was playing with. I took him out of the situation and explained calmly that hands are not for hitting and to say sorry to the little baby boy. We came back in, he said sorry, and it happened again. So I did the same thing again and took him out but this time I explained that if he did it again we would go home. It happened again so this time I had to stick to my guns and take him home. A lovely lady came up to me as I was walking out and said she had seen what happened and that she knew what it was it like - the frustration, tiredness, anxious feelings, as she had a son who went through the same thing. She got hold of me and gave me a massive hug to reassure me that I didn't have the devil child - they all go through their trials and tribulations! I thought it was nice that someone I didn't know could offer support without fear of rejection, just because she could genuinely see how upset I was.

Another Lisa, England

The other morning I went to the garage to get petrol, as I queued to pay I remembered that I needed to buy postage stamps, so when I got to the till I asked the assistant if they sold them. She said they did but didn't have any at the moment. Never mind I thought, and went back to the car. Just as I was about to drive away, the man who had been in the queue behind me walked over to my car and stopped me, he said he had heard me ask to buy stamps and said take this one, handing me a postage stamp. I offered to pay him but he wouldn't let me! So I said thank you and accepted the gift. I thought to myself how nice it was to witness such acts of random kindness, no matter how small they may appear to others. In fact I mentioned it to others that day too, it just made me smile, simple kindness can go such a long way.

Finally a lovely story from my Dad...

To celebrate my 65th birthday this August, I went to America. Following two weeks of travel, my long time friends, Jim and Adele, had asked me to stay with them for my final week. They picked me up from my hotel on Fisherman's Wharf in San Francisco and drove me to their home. I had a fabulous 5 days with them and their two daughters, visiting Lake Tahoe and old town Sacramento. An evening out whilst I was with them became a highlight of my holiday, never to be forgotten.

Jim, who is a young 85 years, is very generous, so to repay their hospitality I insisted that I pay for dinner out for them and their daughter Julie who had assisted in chauffeuring me about.

We dined at Jamie's Bar & Grill on the Broadway in Sacramento. Finishing our main course, Julie suggested that for dessert they take me to Vic's Ice Cream Parlour a few blocks away. Both Jim and I have to keep our sugar intake under control but the temptation was too much as Vic's have made delicious ice cream for two generations.

We parked up and as we opened the door to let Adele and Julie in, two young excited children aged about 6 & 8 charged up followed by mum. "Hold the door for them", she shouted to her children, who stopped in their tracks and both grabbed the door handle to let Jim & I in. Mum said she was always encouraging them to respect their elders. "Oh No"! said Jim, "in you go, please, with your children, before us". I joined in with "Yes! Ice cream shops are for kids. Please let them in first". We followed mum and her children in, then along with Julie & Adele selected from the tempting range of flavours. Once we were seated with our ices, Julie went to pay (they wouldn't let me!).

A few moments later Julie came back to our table to say that someone had paid for our ice creams. It appeared that the mum with the two children had bought their ice creams and paid for us as well before leaving. We could not believe their generosity and this will stay with me forever. What an example that mum set for her children.

We have all experienced random acts of kindness and we are all capable right now of giving them to others. You will feel so excited and energized by your own kind actions. It's such fun! Here are some more ideas...

- Tell someone how great they look, or what a great person they are
- Open doors
- Give away your parking space to someone more in need
- Smile
- Ask a stranger how they are feeling
- Wish everyone well
- Offer something that you have to someone else
- Make cakes and give them to your neighbors
- Offer your time to help someone out
- Baby sit for your friends for free and give them the gift of time
- Spend time with your grandparents and ask them about their lives
- Buy a hat and gloves for a homeless person
- Send your children's old clothes to your local hospital's children's ward
- Give your old magazines and books to a hospice or care home
- Give a hand written letter to someone you care about
- Send thank you cards to all those who give to you
- Leave an extra coin in the vending machine
- Give someone your shopping trolley
- Buy food for those less unfortunate than yourself
- Lend an ear to someone who is having a tough time
- Give your copy of your favorite inspiring book to a friend who needs a lift

- Pay for someone behind you in the drive through
- Share your umbrella with someone who doesn't have one
- Invite someone for dinner who would normally be eating alone
- Be positive to everyone you meet
- Consciously see the best in others and aim to believe in them more than they believe in themselves
- Tell someone a joke
- Read to a child
- Make someone's wish come true
- Do some community work
- Compliment a parent on their child's behavior
- Place a letter in your local news paper thanking others for their acts of kindness

You know it is so easy to be kind, don't be the unkind one

I went to a talk with a wonderful author a few months ago and what some may see as an insignificant, tiny and harmless (it's not) thing happened right before my eyes... We had taken our seats for the first half. Just before the beginning, I sensed a difficult spirit walking up the aisle toward the front of the room. She looked for a place near the front but the seats were all full and disappointedly she walked back to the rear of the hall. Now I must point out that this woman was perfectly able bodied. At the beginning of the second half and after a 30 minute lunch break, people started to wander back to their seats. The same woman stole the seat of someone right before my eyes. When the original woman came to sit back down she had no seat and the new woman ignored her. There were tears of embarrassment in the lady's eyes. Where would she go now? A slight thing to some perhaps but an act of such unkindness! Is this you? Would you do the same?

Don't. You will come here again and again until you learn.

If a man be gracious and courteous to strangers, it shows he is a
citizen of the world, and that his heart is no island cut off from
other lands, but a continent that joins to them.

Francis Bacon

I love others with acceptance

We are all different. We are all unique. We are all self conscious.
We are all anxious that we won't be liked and accepted. Imagine
then what it feels like to someone else when you argue against
them and who they are or what they believe. I am not saying that
there is no room for challenge and debate in some circumstances.
But do we really need to always be the one who is right? To
always feel better? To feel that we are a greater person than
someone else? To compare ourselves and decide that we don't
like someone or the way they look or act, just because they are
different to us?

To take someone and accept who they are and respect what
they believe as their truth is a true gift. We are often so quick to
judge, to make up our minds about someone or something.
Perhaps if we let loose of our ego controlling reins we would be
surprised. People are not always who or what they first appear.
We are all surrounded by people in our lives that are a gift. The
universe revolves around who we are and what we are creating,
whilst magically supporting us in our soul quest in this current
life. Everything happens for a reason and perhaps that person
who you bumped into today and rather wished you had not had
an important message for you. Or was there for you at just the
right time to experience the joy of expressing one of the lessons
or perhaps to experience joy, or kindness or forgiveness, or
acceptance.

We all feel upset when we are judged or excluded. It makes us
upset and feel that we are not good enough, and we become
angry and defensive, or hidden and shy. Think about how you

because with these gifts you are seeking nothing in return. You are truly worthy of love, you will be loved. If you spend your time and energy showing your love to others, purely because that's what you feel, and then give without condition, then your love for yourself will be centered and overwhelming – you will be loving yourself.

When we hold onto a grudge, it eats away at us. The unexpressed hurt and twists of pain affect our physical bodies. You can tell a bitter or angry person just by looking at their faces. Their bodies will also tell you.

After I gave birth to my daughter I couldn't walk properly for two years. I had all sorts of medical tests, physio and scans of my pelvis but nothing could physically be found and the pain continued.

The labour had been good, if a little fast, but when it came to the crunch and I tried for hours to push our daughter into this world, we found that her head was presented in the wrong way for the birth canal, and so it didn't fit. She also had a large head!

The resulting "interference" and c section naturally took its toll on my body. However within a few months, I should have recovered.

Having a daughter brought about emotions and feelings about my relationship with my own mother. A relationship which hasn't always been an easy one, and I thank my mother from the depths of my soul for the sacrifices that she has made for me in her life here, as a soul, to support my learning. Without her enormous gift, this book would never have been created. As a single parent, she worked hard, lost her temper, strove to find her own soul and juggled two young children. Through the depths of despair, through loneliness, through financial insecurity, she faced a future that must have appeared very uncertain at times. I thank her.

So two years after the birth of my own daughter, and on full strength pain killers every day, I was at the end of my tether. One evening I went along to a local school to run a stand at a fund raising evening for women. Beauty therapy, natural therapies, jewellery etc. As a new, enthusiastic coach I went and took a £10 table to see if I could reach some new potential clients for my fledgling coaching business. I didn't, but I did win a prize in the raffle! A free reiki healing session. Off I went and during that session the healer (now a much loved friend) helped me to see the emotional link with my pelvis. It was my relationship with my mother. The years of stored up resentment and anger that were still simmering in my body had found an outlet when my own daughter was born. The pain at times was unbearable.

The wonderful thing with the knowledge that your emotions and feelings have a link to your physical health is that once you find the link and then heal the emotional distress, then the physical disease will heal too. (I have put a few further reading recommendations later on in the book if you would like to read more about the emotional and physical link and healing).

We are constantly re-generating cells in our body. There has to be dis-ease in any of them for them to malfunction, their pain is the method that our body has to awaken our souls to the fact that something emotional has to be done, has to be healed and dealt with.

The weekend after the body mind link was revealed, my mother came to visit. I had to use this visit to let to go of all of the resentment and negative feelings. I had to forgive her in order to heal. To say that it was one of the hardest things that I have ever had to do is a complete understatement. We went for a long walk. We cried. We hugged. We both got very brave. All of the words that had never been said, but so needed to be said, were said.

The next morning I woke up without pain and for the first time in two years I didn't need to take a pain killer. I was healed and I have not experienced any pain in my pelvis since.

I could not argue with this. I had trusted that the emotional link was there. I wanted to get on with my life and I was willing feel when you are misinterpreted because your words are taken out of context or when you are not given a chance to be yourself or voice your truth. Give the gift of acceptance to others. Love them with acceptance. Slow down and consciously try not to judge who they are or what they might be about to say. Listen. If your instincts say spend time with this person or stand and contemplate their words or approach or personality for a moment, then follow those instincts. Be gracious and show others that they can be individual, that they can be themselves and they will take heart in that, just as you would.

Perhaps their negative behavior – or your perception that it is negative is trying to tell you something about an aspect of your life or about your behavior – it may even be a reflection of it.

By the same token, know that you cannot change anyone. Expecting someone to become something that they are not is unkind and soul destroying for them. They cannot be someone that they are not, it will just make them uncomfortable, unhappy and push them away from you. It's a very confusing situation to be in.

When my daughter was three she developed a verucca on her foot. Yes of course she will have picked it up from somewhere, but I was curious what the emotional body link was, so I researched it to find out. The verruca was about anger and frustration. Because I was unsure of the significance of the position on her foot where the verruca was in terms of foot reading and reflexology, I asked a good friend who is a practicing reflexologist. I was shocked and ashamed at the response. The place on the foot represented communication and expression of self. My daughter never stops talking and my husband and I had got to the point where we were finding it difficult to cope with the constant chatter. We had fallen into the trap of getting frustrated and asking her quite frequently to be quiet and stop chattering. I have had her astrological chart done and amongst many gifts that she is here to bring there is one that is above all else in her chart – her gift of expression - HER CHATTER! We had quashed it and as a result she was getting frustrated and the verruca developed!

I felt terrible. My husband and I agreed to try an experiment...to stop asking her to be quiet, unless it was in a situation that really needed her to be quiet. We started straight away. Within 2 days the verruca was gone. It had healed and vanished.

What other people are or are not might bother you. But your being bothered shouldn't be the reason for them to stop being themselves. Take the responsibility to work on your own responses and manage them so that others can express and be who they are.

Give love and unconditional acceptance to those you encounter, and notice what happens.
Wayne Dyer

People are the same in essence, at heart, all throughout their lives but sometimes the roles that we play and the choices that we make give us a few knocks and we fall wakingly unconscious for a time. We zone out, live our beliefs and homogenize for a bit to get through it. Awaken the love and true spirit in others by simply accepting them for who they are, what they have, what they believe and how they live their lives or want to live them. As we get older we unfold. How exciting to find out how interesting and amazing other people can be. It never ceases to astound me how loving and wonderful people are when they step away from the hiding and come out into really being.

Shower people around you with genuine compliments. Tell them how great you think they are. Thank them for their help and for being in your life. Do what you can to show them that they are good enough and they will receive the gift of acceptance. If you find yourself judging and looking someone up and down, gently move into your heart. Compliment them on who they are and give.

To love others with acceptance will show you that the wonder of life is all around you. In your uniqueness, your acceptance of others will unfold the wonders of yourself.

I love others with joy

Let your positivity and love for life light the path for others to find their own joy. See the best in others with love.

The minute some of us start to interact with others, we become negative and sarcastic, putting ourselves, others and the world down, dragging down with us the joy of others and ourselves. Moaning has become the route to common ground! Soap operas, moaning about the boss and whining over a drink or a cigarette have created a negative pattern that influences millions of relationships. If someone is happy and positive we ask what is wrong with them! We may even make them feel odd and guilty for enjoying themselves!

By being negative we are not loving others with joy. Love isn't just reserved for those we live with and our best friends. We have to see everyone as someone important and love them with an open, positive, enjoyment.

Be the one who adds the spark of fun, who loosens the atmosphere. Drop any negative expectations that you have of others. See them as good people doing their best and be friendly. Give enjoyment to others. Have fun!

If we all stand in our groups, at break times, in our homes in the evenings, with smiles on our faces and our focus on the wonderful aspects of the others around us, wouldn't we make a sweeping change in the world! We tend to take for granted those that are closest to us. Those people look to us for their self esteem and acknowledgement that they are good enough. Let's start really showing them that they are. Zone out of the TV and zone in to your children, your wife, your husband, your partner, your son, your daughter, your parent, your friend. Put a smile in your heart and onto your face and take a real interest in what makes them happy. Listen to them. Point out all of the wonderful things that make them themselves. Encourage them to reach for their dreams and reveal the best of themselves.

Sometimes it can be really hard to stay positive, especially when someone we are with is bringing themselves or us down. Know that you can choose your reactions. Stop making everything about you. Listen and keep a positive open heart and help those around you learn their lessons.

Be happy, show others how they make you happy and help to make this world a happier, more joy filled experience.

Every time you smile at someone, it is an action of love, a gift to that person, a beautiful thing.
Mother Teresa

Affirmations for living my life of love

- ♥ I spread love everywhere I go
- ♥ I am kind and generous
- ♥ I share my joy
- ♥ I aim to ignite another's soul
- ♥ My natural state is love
- ♥ I teach love in every moment
- ♥ I choose to be kind
- ♥ I see the best in others
- ♥ I accept others for who they really are

CHAPTER SIX

LIVING LOVE IN LIFE

To each is given a list of rules
A shapeless mass; a bag of tools.
And each must fashion, ere life is flown,
A stumbling block or a stepping stone.
R L Strong

Will you choose to experience advancement in this life or will you deny it? You have the knowledge, your heart knows the tools. No matter where you are in your life right now you can choose to remember, learn and experience the lessons and advance your soul. You can choose to live a life of love.

In life taking back control reveals love

Turn yourself inside out. We are always asking the questions, "What is this all about"? "What should I be doing"? "What is my purpose"? Know that your purpose is right inside you. You should be doing you, being you. Think about your life and reflect on who you really are. If you were to turn your heart inside out and shake it onto the seat where you are sat, what would it look like? What would people see? What would they learn from you?

You can spend decades being someone else, conforming to the rules of society and its social guidelines. You will never experience the knowing of absolute enlightenment until you become truly the person that you are. The one that you were born to be, and you know it.

Every time you blame the world for what you have or haven't got or what you feel has worked against you, you are giving away your control, your power over to others, to circumstances. If you are out of control then you will feel like a victim, powerless in your life. Life will happen to you and all the while you will choose to beat yourself up again and again and again. You will hide and blame and get bitter. If you are out of control you will panic. We wonder why people are mentally and emotionally sick with anxiety and depression and why the world is rattling with anti-depressants. So many people have given their power away. They feel powerless, while life happens all around them and to them. In their eyes it is not their fault. Life has just dealt it to them in this way.

What you can do for yourself and others is to demonstrate that you can be in control. It doesn't matter what has happened to you, or how bad it has been. You can take back your power, embrace the universal laws of love. Remember, experience and learn your lessons. Cherish that absolute knowing that we are all one, that you are a magical part of the whole, that your love, your life is here to create wonder, to create experience, to teach the way.

Listen to your soul and it will show you the way. Hold the love in your heart out there in your life for yourself and the whole world to see. Be brave. Feel the truth in your soul. Take back control.

In life living by your own song strengthens your love

You know the purity of your own heart and mind. Now you have to express it. Not through the doings of someone else but through what you hide. Dare to expose yourself. What you will see is that the vulnerability that is within you is within all of us. We are all scared to reveal that little us inside. The one that we only reveal to those who are very close to us. The loves of our lives, our first loves, those who we have trusted enough to share with abandon. Those people to whom, somehow, we can't help but reveal ourselves, even if we don't want to.

Look back and see the moments when you let go, when you trusted and threw your heart with absolute faith at the universe. When you felt the hurts and threw your anger and "whatever's" to the world, you released your fears. At the times in your life, when it couldn't get any worse. When frustration ripped through your whole being and you gave in, you surrendered. It might have been a "what's the point" or a "here I am again". When the sorrow and pain crowded in, you had only one way to go. To surrender. To surrender to you. To surrender to the universe, to life. To open your heart, cry with pain and surrender to the inner faith of vulnerability. Nothing could make anything worse. You gave up.

When you give in. Capture it. Bottle it. Remember this person. Remember this feeling. This is you. This is the you that you have been searching for, the you that you have been longing to find. Once the hurt begins to create the power, the "I'll show them what I am made of," stick with this you. Write it down. Write out the verses of your song. This is you. Vulnerable, wonderful you. Those dreams that you have at these moments are what you are. Live them. Don't let society or others create a free fall back into the numbing world of doing and keeping up with those around you. Don't go and buy "stuff", don't find out what the latest thing is on TV so that you can follow it and be in the know. Let it all go!

So many of us shut down with pain. By shutting down you are shutting down the real you. By turning your back and cheek and denying the pain and the hurt, you are saying no to an amazing, soul-confirming experience. By standing and facing the pain, no matter how hard and embarrassing it is, you find yourself. Turn towards the pain. Live the hurt for whatever it takes and experience a gift that life has brought for you to find yourself again. To grow and move beyond your safe boundaries. Throw yourself at the pain and with tender care to yourself journey to see what is revealed, knowing that you will survive.

The people in your life who have allowed you to feel this, whether it ended in hurt or not, were a true gift. Don't ever forget that feeling. Try to find it again. Place yourself in a dream state and imagine what your life will be when you let go and live that lovely dream. Forget the money, the "stuff". Go for the feeling. This is your answer. This is what will make you happy.

Do whatever you need to do to lift your energy. For me music is the key, it aligns my faith in love. For some it's reading, poetry, walking, playing with their kids, watching the sunset. When was the last time that you opened your door, walked out into the cold night, sat down and looked up at the stars? Do it. Do it today. Do what lifts your spirit. You will feel magical, connected, grounded. You are the very best of everything that you will ever be. So be it now. Trust it.

We are all centered in love. You don't have to experience pain to find it. Joy does the same thing. Joy has the power to reveal the wonders of the world, your world to you, in exactly the same feeling. As souls we all have a unique gift to bring to ourselves and the world. Start to reveal yours by living the lessons through your own song.

Be strong. Take hold of the reins of the soul and celebrate the end of the cycle for you, your coming of age. Make a promise right now to trust and surrender with love. What is the worst that can happen? You love yourself more and make more friends? What's the best that can happen? When you leave this dimension you will have done it. You will have experienced it. You will have been it. You will have given it.

Your song is forgiveness. Your song is kindness. Your song is acceptance. Your song is Joy.

Have no regrets, become the light that you are.

In life every thought causes an effect

You are what you believe. Thoughts become things. If you look at your life and want more, want a better experience, then consciously decide to begin experiencing that change now. When I started my business I had a tough few years. I went from earning a lot of money to earning none. My ego took a few knocks and I was in the habit of comparing my successes to what I had and my balance sheet. Three years on I sat on a beach for the first time in five years, stared out to sea and decided that life was going to change. I opened my heart and listened to my soul. What did I really want to create? Who was I and what did I need to follow, which road should I choose to express who I really was. I found that when I felt like me, deep within, sat looking at those waves, that I felt an elation, a power that lifted my spirit and made me excited and bubbling with love. When I dreamt of doing something that exposed my soul, my love to the world, then I felt powerful, not in a leadership sense but in an emotional one. I wanted to create a life that felt like what I imagined it must feel like to be a singer who has written a song of love and belts it out to millions on stage. Love at high intensity, pouring from the heart. I can't sing, I can't play music. So where should I start?

If thoughts become things, I realised sat on that beach that this life of ours can be exactly what we make of it. I had no money in the bank. I had no idea where my business was going. I knew that life was there to be created. I had an excitement within me that I had never felt before. I felt totally in control.

I began to dream. Watching the clouds move across the sky I imagined in my mind that I was doing that thing, being that person who was pouring out all of their heart to excite and warm up the world and everyone they met. I felt a happiness that had been missing whilst I had been caught up in my panicking and doing.

I started to manifest.

When I returned home everything had changed. I chose to know that the world would unfold in the way it should. I chose to see that only good would come. I chose to know that the phone would ring when it should, that I would be strong and successful in whatever way that the universe dealt. This doesn't mean sitting back and waiting for life to happen. The best of what life has to offer is expressing itself in your life right now. Know it, create it, be it.

Know that the phone will ring for you, that opportunities will present themselves with perfect timing. Books and knowledge will unfold. Choose lighter days, days where you are open to love.

We are all part of this amazing flow of life, this universal pattern of perfection. The threads that our thoughts and emotions weave create the reality of our lives. We begin by awakening and then choosing to know that love and happiness and goodness and everything that we need are here right now in our lives. All of the answers are already within us. We act and know and think as if because as if, is.

If you need help ask for it. Before I had the mystical vision I connected with the prayer of St Francis. "Make me a channel of your peace" was everywhere in my life. I dreamt about it. I sang it in the shower. It filled my days and nights. It was answered. Ask. Every question causes an effect. Often the answers are from within so you need to listen to your own heart and inner visions and feelings and follow what feels right. Stop looking outside for your answers and look within, when you listen, the truth will be revealed. "Let him who has ears hear" The Gospel of Thomas.

In life love holds power

You are an amazing powerful instrument of love. You have the power to heal, to create, to transform. I have lain in bed feeling a cold descend upon me. A throat with a slight itch. The beginnings of sinus pain. That sitting on a cloud like feeling that you get when you begin to feel under the weather. I have then laid there and known that I was healthy and well. I have known that

I am rested. I do not need the break that an illness would bring. Life is a break. I am happy. I look after myself. I have space and calm and time and everything is right and perfect in my life. When I do this, the colds never come.

This universe is like a vehicle. We can control it beyond what we believe right now and we start with ourselves. If you think that life happens to you, that it is all bad, that people will always let you down, that you will never be loved, guess what. That's right, you will get exactly what you know. When you choose the path of love and enlighten to yourself, you and everything that comes to you will be because of you. With love not fear, life will become even greater and even greater and even greater.

Your personality will never really be ready for what your soul
wants to achieve in this life.
Dr Robert Holden

Drop your fearful thoughts and center yourself in love. Feel excited because it is time for your soul to step forward. My soul knows, right now, that there will be people all over the world that will read these words and find comfort and hope and love from them. My insecurity screams no, no. But my soul is much greater than any fear that my personality might hold. Feel the power of your love and intention. Feel it in yourself now, your soul reacts in harmony to who you are.

Feel your power. You will find it in your love. Every thought, every emotion that you have has an effect. Make your wishes wisely. Do not focus upon what you don't want. Know what you are creating and being and then be and experience that in your consciousness right now. Bring it all into now. Let your imagination become your current consciousness, whilst enjoying the present and live your wildest dreams. You are here to live in your joy through your choice to create and express joy. Do this whilst living the lessons and you will advance your soul.

In life your love can influence the whole world

Just as manifestation has power for you, know it also has an effect for others and that as a group our consciousness is affected by your individual thoughts and levels of love.

When you live your life in love, as well as loving yourself and others through forgiveness, kindness, acceptance and joy, you are also manifesting for others. At a great level, you are raising your consciousness beyond awakening, you as an individual have the power when you express your soul to influence group consciousness. You can see this right now with your impact upon your family and their lives and experience. What you feel and think rubs off. You are contagious. If you choose to be yourself and take control and be happy and positive, your family unit does too. You build a culture, a feeling and a reality.

If you can influence here, you can influence at greater levels. We are all so powerful. If we collectively live in love in greater and greater numbers, we will influence world consciousness. The ripple effects of you cause cascades of happiness – if you allow them to.

As my favorite, Barry Manilow, sings, it all starts "with one voice singing in the darkness" and soon "the whole world will sing".

You have the power to begin and continue a chain reaction of love that goes all around this world and beyond it. You are love. So be it. Take a conscious active role through your own advancement to support others in theirs. We will wake up the world. Encourage love and kindness in yourself, in your children, in your schools, in your offices, in your homes, in your counties, in your continent, in your world.

Live love in life by manifesting on greater and greater levels by starting the ignition with your own beautiful spark.

In life grace is the faith of the loving

When it all gets too much, simply throw it all back and wait for the answer. You can never be wrong when you are centered in you. The universe will provide you with everything that you need. If you get the wrong thing then you have lost your center. Your clue is your emotions. If you are angry, frustrated, then you are going about it the wrong way. Instead of putting pen to paper and trying to logically "work out" the universe, ask for help through your heart and let it go. Have faith that everything is as it should be. That it will all be okay.

> Your impulses are the grace for you to respond to.
> Caroline Myss

Have faith that **truly being you and revealing you is enough.** It is. It is all that is asked from you. When my grandmother died she said to my father "say goodbye to them". She left with nothing, just as she had arrived. My other grandmother, my Nanny, spent years not knowing who she was or who we were, she had dementia. Do you think that what she owned mattered? What will you do with all of your "stuff" and "doings" when you go from here? You can't take any of that with you. What you do take is your love, your experiences. If you don't have any because you are caught up in a world of doing and collecting, then change it. Right now. Look around and see where you can help. Have faith that whatever you know is there to truly help yourself and also the people around you that you meet. You assist in enabling them to experience love and all of the wonderful lessons of this life, simply by being yourself and trusting your truth.

Go for your dreams. Never sit still if you want to keep experiencing. Tune in now and again and experience the conversations of your soul through silence and enjoyment of simply listening to you. Aim to have a life of experience that you will never forget.

One that you throw yourself at. You could have done nothing more. You never held yourself back.

When you allow it, your soul speaks. We all have huge moments of self doubt. The trick is not to stay there forever, but to trust and have faith that as human beings and spiritual, energy beings, we have these experiences for a reason - to show us that we can slow down with the doing, the showing and that we can then just be. That it's okay not to look around and know the answer.

"Let go and let god". It works every time. Just like "what would love do"?

It's when we let go and have faith that miracles happen. When we hold who we are in our hearts and where we want to go. We feel the magic, the vulnerability, the letting go. We sleep on it. We trust that the answer will come. That god, the universe, will deliver. We know that we are loved, that we are never alone. We just know that the right words will come. Have faith that inspiration will guide you.

Be ready, for some will scorn your approach. Others will simply stop wanting to be with you. Others will laugh and turn the other cheek. Know that you are here for you. To experience you. Have faith. Don't conform. Stick your neck out and stick to your guns. Show them what you are made of. Carve your own direction. Have faith that this is enough. Those who have promised will support you, they will come to you and surround you.

Be you. Have faith. This is all that you need.

In life your greatest tool is your essence and your power of choice to be happy

Look after yourself. Loving yourself is one huge step towards supporting your advancement, but without a focus, a choice to be positive every day, the journey can knock you off purpose.

When negativity and challenge are thrown at you, choose to see and experience it positively. If you are stressed and down, then this low feeling will cloud your vision of the wonder of now and all of the opportunities that are there for the taking.

Choose to experience activities that you enjoy. The happier that you can feel day to day the better. You will be more open to your soul and your path. Positivity is very important throughout your awakening. It is the loving seat belt that will protect your fragile self from all of the bumps and knocks along the way. It is a mental state. A choice. Of all of the work that I have done on my own learnings in life and development, staying positive has been the thing that has supported me consistently to be powerful and reach ahead. It has helped me to be open to change and transition. Something that we all tend to face as we begin to unveil our selves, unwrap the paper and start to decipher who we are.

By reading this book you have made a conscious choice to journey into the unknown. And yet this unknown is actually the known. You just don't remember it. For some the changes that then occur as we move towards our great awakening can be life changing. They can call into question every relationship that you have ever had. Thoughts and ideas and ways of living that you have thought for years were the right way suddenly become the wrong way and you end up wondering why you never knew!

As you emerge to find your true self and give yourself to you and the world, some of the people that surround you will fall away. For some they are simply not ready for this step yet. They need more time. They just can't see it. Be compassionate and let them go. To do this you need positivity, day to day. It can feel lonely at first when you spend time with yourself. Self doubt can creep in when others question who we are as we emerge. Remember that you are not changing in any real sense, you are simply becoming yourself. If you have spent many years asleep in the doing then some of the people around you will not recognize the you underneath. Take your learnings from the previous chapters and apply positive choice to your everyday reactions to protect yourself from the bumps.

As long as there are people not ready to express what you are reading in your hands then there will be negativity and doubt in the world.

Just because others see things negatively doesn't mean that you have to. Stand back and be happy in your own thoughts. It might mean that you feel alone at times and this can make you self conscious. Be ready for new people to warm to you however, who you never knew existed in your circle before your awakening. As you become more of yourself and are happy and positive throughout your days you will attract like minded people. Enjoy these new relationships and choose not to be drawn into the past with negativity and comparisons.

Here are a selection of my tips to support your day to day positivity...

- Know what makes you cross and procrastinate and manage it. Avoid the people that pull you down and choose to spend your time with positive people.
- Manage what you absorb into your consciousness. Your mind cannot tell the difference between TV when you are really "in" to it, when you could be sat on the moon in your own living room, and reality. So if you are watching violent films, or negative soap operas, know that your mind believes that they are your reality.
- Promote positivity be speaking kindly throughout your day. Always put a positive slant on things.
- When you start to feel down, instead of pressing self destruct, be kind to yourself and change what you are doing to something that you enjoy. It might be reading. It might be music. This isn't about avoiding the challenges, it is about bringing yourself up so that you can view your reality with perspective, rather than fear.

- Go for a walk.
- Sleep on it. If something is troubling you it can generally wait until the next morning or this afternoon. Let it lie and trust that your subconscious mind will give you the solution, more often than not the right words and resolutions will come.
- Wait before you react. Step back and diffuse your emotions before you respond to negativity or challenges.
- Exercise. Physical activity lifts your feel good hormones and gives you energy.
- Eat well and don't overload on sugar. The ups and downs that come with it will affect your moods. Have a treat now and again instead and look after your body. It houses your soul.
- Sit up straight and smile.
- Use colour to lift your moods. Avoid veiling yourself in beige and black. Choose vibrant colours. Having fantastic underwear will boost your confidence and make you smile, male or female!
- Take time on your journeys. Know that a few minutes won't make a difference and get to your destination in a relaxed, happy frame of mind.
- Know how lucky you are.
- Ban the word "why" from your vocabulary. Is makes others feel attacked and challenged. It's very personal. You will avoid defensive attitudes and emotions by replacing it with a "what". Change this simple habit and it will positively change your relationships forever. It works wonders with everyone, especially your partner and children.

Fear less, hope more; Eat less, chew more; Whine less, breathe more; Talk less, say more; Love more, and all good things will be yours.
Swedish Proverb

In life your body speaks the language of your soul

If you were looking for the magic pill that will instantly give you answers to where you are right now, then know that you are sat right in it. Your body is highly attuned to your soul. Your emotions and thoughts, your behaviors and environments all affect your body. The human body is an instrument to enlightenment. Listen to it. Any illness, any discomfort, any ache, any pain is a message that something is out of balance and a change in approach is required. You can use your body as a measure of where you are in your path of love, to yourself, to others and in your life.

I highly recommend books by Louise Hay, David Hamilton and Deb Shapiro, if you would like to find out more about this fascinating subject. Know that as I have demonstrated earlier in my life, you can choose to heal yourself. But you can also choose to use your present physical state as an instant daily indicator of your emotional, mental and spiritual health. If you have a cold, are you giving yourself enough rest or have you cried the tears that need shedding? If my sinuses are getting blocked, I know that I am mentally taking on too much. If I get a runny tummy I know that I am either very upset about something or I have been rushing. A sore throat, what are you not saying, expressing? Painful stiff knees, what do you fear about your future? Shoulders sore? What burdens are you carrying? Earache? What do you not want to hear?

In general your left side indicates the females in your life and your emotions and feelings. Your right side represents the men in your life and money, work, the doing of life. Start to diagnose yourself. Your feet are also a great indicator because as the healing power of reflexology illustrates, each part of the foot represents a different part of the body. Each part of the body represents an emotional aspect of yourself, your relationships and your life. Investigate it. It's amazing.

As you move along your loving path you will become heightened in vibration and so will be able to pick up energy from other people and from objects and environments. Some things, some people you will instantly feel comfortable or uncomfortable with. The human being is an amazingly powerful thing. If a dog can sense fear, imagine what you can sense. You can use your intuitive reactions to energy to inform you in your approaches. You also however need to manage negative energy, which as you become more sensitive, you can absorb. You can clear your energy with water. Take a shower or a bath. You can call upon Archangel Michael and Saint Germain to help you to cut cords of negative energy. When you experience negative energy either by being within the presence of others or in low vibe feeling places shield yourself with an invisible force field. Intent is a very powerful thing. Know that you can shield yourself from it and you will.

Dowsing is another good way of checking your energy. Buy yourself a pendulum from a holistic shop and hold it over your seven chakras. (see illustration below). My Reiki Master taught

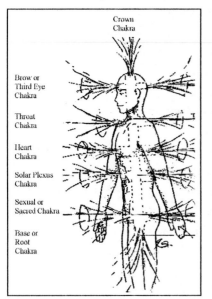

Crown Chakra

Brow or Third Eye Chakra

Throat Chakra

Heart Chakra

Solar Plexus Chakra

Sexual or Sacred Chakra

Base or Root Chakra

me that if the pendulum spins in a clockwise circle then the energy of the chakra is good. If the pendulum swings from side to side know that the chakra is closed and use crystals, energy healing like reiki or actions in yourself and your life to open up the energy in that chakra. If your pendulum swings up and down the body vertically when you are lying down then your chakra energy is directed at source. Good in the crown chakra if you are channelling but elsewhere what have you given up on? Where in the universe have you thrown your power. A swing to the left or right shoulder indicates the male and female energies that I mentioned earlier. These will give you clues to the actions that you need to take in your life and approaches to create a healthy spinning chakra. To the left, which females are influencing you, which feelings and emotions are involved? To the right, which men are influencing you or is it work or money or housing and shelter that is bothering or negatively influencing you? By playing I have since found that if you hold a pendulum over someone's heart chakra and ask them to say negative things about themselves or feel their fears, their heart chakra closes. Conversely, as they say positive things about themselves or fill their heart with love, their heart chakra opens!

I have been testing healing myself with love. It started one night when I woke up with a sore shoulder. No matter how much I tried to ignore it the pain would not go away. I really needed to sleep. I lay in my bed and imaged engulfing the whole area with love. I centred my awareness in my heart and really expanded that loving feeling and in my mind's eye placed that love into every cell of my shoulder. It worked. I was amazed. I fell asleep and the next morning my shoulder felt fine.

Recently my daughter developed a sore eye. The eye was red and weeping slightly. It was evening and we had no antiseptic drops in the house and so I decided to try it with her. At bedtime I suggested that she filled her heart with love and imaged washing her eye with it. I suggested that she asked God and the angels to wash her eye with love now and throughout the night whilst she slept. She did. The next morning the eye was so much better. She kept imagining and asking and by bedtime that following day the eye was completely back to normal. Try it!

Listen to your body and act on your intuition and the guidance that it is telling you. Follow it each time you feel any dis-ease and you will begin to instantly recognize when something is up.

You then have the power to change it and get back on track.

Whilst you are at it become curious as to why certain things happen to you in your life, what are they trying to teach you. Everything happens for a reason. When you look back in your life there were certain things that happened to you that at the time you couldn't understand, but now looking back they make perfect sense because without that thing happening to you, you wouldn't have done this or that or met that person or found that missing link. Sometimes these things come through our intuition.

At the age of eighteen and the week before I was due to start at university, I was away on holiday in France. I had a dream that I should switch universities, cities. I rang my mother and told her that I HAD to change and go to Manchester instead. It was a very powerful forced feeling. To my amazement my mother said fine and offered to call them and try to arrange some accommodation for me (I thought she'd go mad, but sometimes those around us are set up to react a certain way to support our life path). I went to Manchester and in my final year I met my wonderful husband, an amazing, kind and very wise soul who constantly surprises me with his power, wisdom and deep knowledge.

Sometimes dramatic changes and events can come from life with a shock to show you a new way or in my case to stop you in your tracks. You attract everything in your life and some of that attraction is your subconscious and higher self, your soul, lining good and occasionally challenging circumstances up to support you on your path to advancement.

Last summer I was at home and wanted to drop off a birthday present for a friend. She was at her mother's farm. Now I am not good with animals. I am not sure why but dogs, especially large ones, make me nervous and on this farm there are lots of them. I had never been to the farm but all of my instincts cringed at the thought of going there and being around the animals. But, my daughter wanted to go and I dearly wanted to give my friend her birthday present. I pushed my fears aside, against all of my own inner wisdom. My friend called and encouraged me that it would be fine. I had been here before many years before as a teenager, with different people and different circumstances, but there in a situation that I knew I felt uncomfortable in, but to please and not be seen to be silly, I put my fears aside and did what others wanted, I conformed. What an idiot I was. I hadn't fallen into this trap for a long time. Since sitting on the beach I mentioned earlier I act on nothing but my intuition!

Off we went to the farm. We dropped off the present. The animals made me nervous and I begged a hasty retreat. I felt completely out of my comfort zone. On the way back home in the car I came towards a corner and coming in the other direction was a car far too wide and too fast. It went straight into us. A head on collision, it wrote off my car. I will never forget the searing pain of the whiplash and the cry of my daughter's scream when we stopped.

Luckily we escaped with pain for a few weeks and bruises. Immediately I knew why this had happened to us. The universe had sent me a very strong message that that old behavior of conforming against my better judgment has to STOP. I heard the message. Forgave myself and the young lad coming the other way and moved on. I am however even more resolute and clear that I will not compromise my intuition again.

That inner knowing that you have is generally always right. Do not ignore it. Use it as a tool to live love in life. Trust that it is all knowing.

In life seek loving support

There are a growing body of people who are starting to move towards the path of love in life. Many though are not yet at this stage and the challenge remains for us all individually to find this path all whilst living amongst a group in our societies who are caught up in the doing, the ego, the negatives and the fear. To find and follow the path of living love in life we need support. It's okay to seek help. You don't have to do this alone. You are not alone. No matter where you live, with a little research you will find like minded souls on their own journey of advancement. The comfort of finding these lovely amazing and inspirational people brings comfort beyond measure. The spiritual path is a beautiful one but one where you may need little fuel ups of inspiration to keep you on track. Some souls come here to help and support others. Many call these people light workers. They are here to support your path and those of others.

You may be the only one in your family who is instinctively drawn to finding out more about yourself and spiritual truth and that can be a challenging and lonely position. By seeking out, supporting and leaning on others in the same situation we collectively grow and learn. I have met some truly amazing people. All of whom have contributed to my path in ways beyond their own imagination.

Whatever your natural pull, seek out help and immerse yourself in support.

That first day on the beach I pulled my first daily angel card. I have chosen a card every day since and there has not been one day when I have not taken in and been guided by its message. For me these cards are lovingly supportive. I feel comfortable with them. I have guidance through astrology which has been accurate beyond imagination and I continue to investigate spiritual truth through the stars, the power of crystals, the knowledge of colour, energy and its influence and synergies.

Read. There are shelves of amazing texts available in the world, a growing body of knowledge on a vast range of subjects. New and emerging discoveries are being made about heart based living and compassion, the power of the heart, the striking truth about mediumship, healing and manifestation. Take comfort and let the words of other souls light your own path.

Follow your curiosity and trust that you, that love, will find its way.

In life you are never alone, you are always part of the greater truth

We all want to know the truth of this life. In this book I have shared it as I was shown it. The people that I meet all want to have such a divine connection. I believe that we can all experience being connected to our greater truth because as I look back on my own life and the years and months leading up to the experience what I now realize is that there was a method to opening up my spirit to divine connection. If I can do it you can do it. And so I have listed below the stages that I believe that I went through to open up the channel. Try it and let me know what mystical experiences you have.

Step one - **Surrender**, stop controlling everything in your life and directly throw your life with love at source. This doesn't mean doing nothing, but it does mean not fretting if nothing is happening. Accept what is as the flow that is right for your life right now and act on any hunches. Let go and let god. Ask the universe what it wants you to do today, right now, this minute and trust and act on the answer.

Step two - **Ask.** Ask to receive direction. In your heart tell source that you are ready to be a channel for peace. Know that you are being heard and start a conversation going with your guides and source with love, another way of putting this would be to pray.

Step three - **Don't push.** Let go of the future. Listen to your own inner voice and the words and circumstances around you and get on with enjoying your life.

Step four - **Be happy.** Work to follow your joy. Do what you want, not what you should.

Step five - **Work on your issues**. Forgive yourself and others. Set them and yourself free. If you need to see a therapist to uncoil your pains then do. Write down all of your grievances and resentments and hold the intention to let them go. Use the forgiveness process on page 67 of this book to set yourself free. Have an emotional fresh start and walk forward in your life.

Step six - **Love who you are. Be who you are**. Know that who you are is good enough. Accept who you are and show yourself to the people around you. Feel the relief of taking off the mask that you simply no longer need.

Step seven - **Be positively grateful.** Choose to see the positive in everything. Only have positive thoughts about yourself and others. Open up the doorway to your soul, your crown and your third eye to receiving messages.

Step eight - **Work on boosting your intuition**. Meditate. Train in Reiki. Use Angel cards. Remain open.

Then LOVE. Get on with your life and don't waste a minute. If we truly knew everyday the truth of who we really are we would not hesitate to give love into everything to the fullest of our capacity. We would just go for it! So choose your direction and set sail. From this moment decide to love and advance your soul.

Affirmations for living my life of love

- ♥ My strength is created by my love
- ♥ I let go and let love flow
- ♥ I am doing it, I am being love in every moment
- ♥ I create the love that flows into my life
- ♥ I am a powerful source of love
- ♥ I use my love to heal
- ♥ I enjoy the present and live my wildest dreams!
- ♥ I am so powerful, through love I influence at greater and greater levels
- ♥ I experience all of the wonderful lessons of this life
- ♥ I never hold myself back, love moves me forward
- ♥ It is ok to seek help
- ♥ I am in direct connection with our truth

A NEW AGE

By living love in life you are joining a new world age. We are entering a new era of humanity, life on this planet, life as an experience, as a collection of souls. We are moving away from being a world centered on the self and moving into an age where love will reveal itself as the answer, leaving fear behind. I look forward with enormous excitement to the natural, real discoveries that we will make.

Our world's religions are being evaluated and reviewed with new eyes. Their deep messages resonate with us but perhaps their directive traditions and the approach of their worship will be called into question. Those that are centered in heart and there for the greater good may remain. Those that have selfishness and the promotion of fear at their heart may in time be exposed.

Our governments are slowly waking up to the idea that there can be a different way to governing the world. New world leaders are emerging whose way of living is more authentic, more loving, more focused in peace than war.

More and more books are being written on abundance, on the law of attraction. We are no longer burning our mediums and healers at the stake. Their acceptance is bringing in a new age of openness to opportunity, openness to a new power, a power of universal proportions.

More and more of us are meditating. The ancient scripts like the Tao, The Course of Miracles, are being brought forth to us for a reason...to support our awakening and our subsequent opening to living through love.

The world is being awoken. My wish is that these words will help you to awaken to your own truth. You are love. You have this amazing chance right now to advance your soul.

Step into your free will and choose it.

Our prayer of St Francis

I am a channel of peace.
Where there is hatred, I bring my love.
Where there is injury, my pardon.
And where there's doubt, true faith in love:

I choose that I will never seek;
So much to be consoled as to console;
To be understood as to understand;
To be loved, as to love with all my soul.

I am a channel of peace.
Where there's despair in life, I bring hope;
Where there is darkness, only light;
And where there's sadness, ever joy:

I am a channel of peace.
It is in pardoning that I am pardoned,
In giving of myself that I receive,
And in dying that I am born to eternal life.

We are all pencils in the hand of God.
Mother Teresa

BOOKS

O is a symbol of the world, of oneness and unity. In different cultures it also means the "eye," symbolizing knowledge and insight. We aim to publish books that are accessible, constructive and that challenge accepted opinion, both that of academia and the "moral majority."

Our books are available in all good English language bookstores worldwide. If you don't see the book on the shelves ask the bookstore to order it for you, quoting the ISBN number and title. Alternatively you can order online (all major online retail sites carry our titles) or contact the distributor in the relevant country, listed on the copyright page.

See our website www.o-books.net for a full list of over 500 titles, growing by 100 a year.

And tune in to myspiritradio.com for our book review radio show, hosted by June-Elleni Laine, where you can listen to the authors discussing their books.

mySpiritRadio

Read more about your Awakening and Advancing Your Soul on
Elizabeth's website
www.elizabethvillani.net
Use the contact page to send in your stories of your awakening
and journeys of advancement to Elizabeth (I'd love to hear
them)
Namaste

www.fundsforjoy.com

A percentage of the profits made from this book is donated to
the non profit making social enterprise Funds For Joy begun by
Elizabeth in 2010. Funds for Joy exists to warm up the world by
spreading happiness in our world and helping those in need to
reveal the love and happiness within themselves. To do this
important work Funds For Joy needs support. If you have
enjoyed this book and would like to give back to the world or
would simply like to find out more about how you can support
Funds For Joy or get involved yourself then please visit the
website at www.fundsforjoy.com

Together we can spread the love.